Decorating Cakes for Fun and Profit

Decorating Cakes
For Fun and Profit

RICHARD V. SNYDER

Owner and Instructor of the Snyder
School of Cake Decoration, Detroit, Michigan

ILLUSTRATED

AN EXPOSITION-BANNER BOOK

EXPOSITION PRESS   SMITHTOWN, NEW YORK

OTHER BOOKS BY RICHARD V. SNYDER
PUBLISHED BY EXPOSITION PRESS

27 *Special Creations for Cake Decorators*
28 *More Floral Creations for Cake Decorators*
65 *Buttercream Flowers*
29 *New Floral Creations for Cake Decorators*

Second Printing, January, 1955
Third Printing, November, 1957
Fourth Printing, December, 1957
Fifth Printing, March, 1960
Sixth Printing, April, 1960
Seventh Printing, April, 1960
Eighth Printing, June, 1963
Ninth Printing, July, 1963
Tenth Printing, August, 1963
Eleventh Printing, January, 1966
Twelfth Printing, February, 1966
Thirteenth Printing, March, 1972
Fourteenth Printing, August, 1975
Fifteenth Printing, May, 1979
Sixteenth Printing, January, 1983

FIRST EDITION

© 1953 by Richard V. Snyder

Library of Congress Catalog Card Number: 53-8517

ISBN 0-682-40088-2

Printed in the United States of America

To the memory of my father

GEORGE L. SNYDER

*a first-class tradesman
and a fine citizen*

Foreword

This book is for beginners, boys and girls, men and women, hobbyists and tradespeople. Read the book and look at the pictures first. Then get your materials together and start with Chapter I. Do the exercises in order, because each one helps you do the ones that follow.

The illustrations are numbered consecutively throughout the book. Some have several parts which are lettered for easy reference. For instance, 30D refers to the fourth step in basket-weaving in illustration number thirty.

Students and professional decorators will find the volume useful as a handbook and reference work. The index and calendar of decorating ideas at the back of the book will prove helpful in finding particular items.

This volume is intended to be the first in a series. Later volumes will use the same basic techniques and principles which are taught here; they will merely expand their application to secure a greater variety of work.

Grateful acknowledgment is made to the Michigan Consolidated Gas Company for the home-tested recipes which their Home Service Department contributed to Chapter X, and to Mr. William C. Tucker, Grossman-Knowling Company, Detroit, who did all the excellent photography.

R. V. S.

Contents

Decorating Cakes for Fun and Profit

I

Materials and Tools

MAKING BUTTER CREAM DECORATING ICING

Materials: Vegetable Shortening (kept at room temperature)
Powdered Sugar (Icing Sugar)
(fine-ground and free of hard lumps)
Eggs, Vanilla, Salt (fine-ground)

Tools: Mixing Bowl, Mixing Spoon, Rubber or Plastic
Kitchen Spatula, Measuring Cups, Measuring
Spoons, Sifter (fine-mesh)

Empty into a mixing bowl a one-pound can of vegetable
shortening (kept at room temperature), *or* measure 2 level cups
of vegetable shortening and put them in mixing bowl.

Measure 2 level cups of fine-ground powdered sugar (icing
sugar) and *sift* them into mixing bowl.

Without whipping air into them mix ingredients slowly until
they become a smooth blend.

Separate egg whites from yolks. Measure ¼ cup egg white
and add it to mixing bowl.

Add 1 teaspoon vanilla, or to taste, depending upon quality

and strength of vanilla. Without incorporating air into it, blend mixture slowly and thoroughly.

Measure 2 level cups of powdered sugar and ¾ teaspoon fine-ground salt, and *sift* them into mixing bowl.

Without whipping air into them, mix ingredients slowly until they become a smooth blend.

Notes: The vegetable shortening (such as Crisco, Spry, etc.) must be at room temperature when it is used. It must be very pliable.

Butter may be substituted for a third of the shortening if a butter flavor is desired. The butter must be at room temperature and it must be thoroughly blended with the shortening before any powdered sugar is added. Use ½ teaspoon salt instead of ¾ teaspoon. The icing that results will not be as white as the 100% shortening icing, and it will be a little softer. If it is too soft, sift a little more powdered sugar into the batch and blend carefully until it is smooth.

There are variations in the dryness of sugar and the consistency of shortening at different times of the year and in different parts of the country. If heat and humidity are extremely high, it may be necessary to add four or more tablespoons of sifted corn starch. Ordinarily, if the icing is too soft for your purpose, add a small amount of sifted powdered sugar as necessary. If the batch is too stiff, add more egg white or a few drops of water.

The icing should not be aerated at all. It should have the smooth consistency of very soft putty. It should flow easily from the cone and still retain its shape.

A large, commercial-sized recipe in pounds and ounces is included in Chapter X, p. 122.

When the icing is mixed, put it in a plastic or metal container, or a wide-mouthed jar that can be tightly closed. If the air is kept from the icing, it will remain smooth.

Store the icing in a cool part of the kitchen, pantry, or basement stairway. It will then be ready for use at any time. Do not store it in the refrigerator unless room temperature is above 90 degrees F. When stored properly, a butter and shortening icing will keep for weeks; a 100% shortening icing will keep for months.

Many other food substances can be used successfully for decorating cakes, cookies, petit fours, pies, ice cream, salads, sandwiches, appetizers, meat dishes, eggs, and fish. Among them are royal icing (see Chapter X, p. 124), Philadelphia Cream Cheese, whipped cream, meringue, salad dressing, mashed potatoes, butter, meat pastes, mashed and sieved hard-boiled egg yolks mixed with salad dressing. (Ceramists find that even clay can be worked successfully with tubes.)

It is best, however, to use butter cream icing during the learning stage because it is more convenient to store and easier to handle. As you master basic techniques, you can experiment with materials other than butter cream.

After you remove a portion of the icing for immediate use, be careful to close the storage container at once, so that the main batch of icing will remain smooth indefinitely.

In order to use this icing, we shall need some paper cones.

MAKING PAPER CONES

Cut parchment paper into squares that are approximately twelve inches on each side. Cut squares diagonally to form triangles. Place papers so that the long sides are facing to your right. Mark an X at middle point of long side.

With your left hand bend farthest corner of paper toward you in such a way that your fingers are wrapped inside and your thumb is on top of the paper. (Fig. 1.)

Continue turning left hand toward you until cone is formed with point at X.

With fingers of left hand still inside cone, and palm of right hand down, place forefinger under lower right corner of paper. Place second finger of right hand above the same corner. (Fig. 2.)

Bring right hand up, over, and under, to complete the cone. Pull right hand toward you in order to form a sharp point. (Fig. 3.)

Figure 1

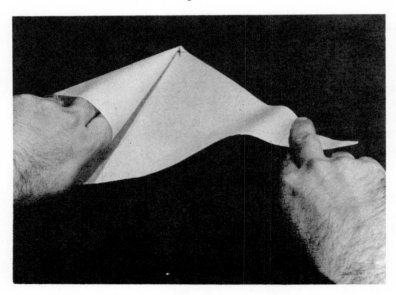

Figure 2

Grasp cone at outside seam between thumb and index finger of right hand, and remove left hand from cone. (Fig. 4.)

With both hands fold high points of cone top once or twice. Tear folded edge at two places, about one-half inch apart, and fold ribbon of paper downward to keep cone from coming apart at the top. (Fig. 4.)

Notes: Several cones can be made up in advance for later use.

If paper cone is too narrow, spread fingers of left hand before removing it from completed cone.

It is important that cones have sharp points. Merely pull paper toward you with right hand before removing left hand from cone.

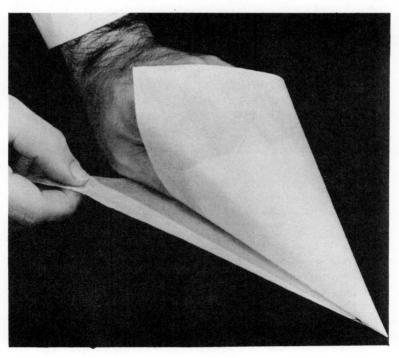

Figure 3

Figure 4

You can purchase rolls or sheets of parchment paper in large department stores or bakery supply houses. If you cannot obtain parchment readily, use a good grade of waxed paper or wrapping paper, or even paper sacks. It may be necessary to use a cone of waxed paper inside a cone of wrapping paper if the paper is of poor quality.

If you already know how to form a good cone from a triangular or rectangular piece of paper, disregard the previous instructions. The main thing is to be able to make a good cone quickly and efficiently.

At one time or another you may have bought a decorating set in a department store. The set probably contained several metal or plastic points, plus a metal or fabric device for holding the icing. Naturally you would like to use them.

USING METAL TUBES

Paper cones can be used exclusively until Chapter III. You are advised, however, that metal tubes (sometimes called tips or points) used in conjunction with paper cones will make your work easier, more varied, and more professional.

The following metal tubes* should be obtained in the near future from a bakers' wholesale supply house if you have not already bought them: plain tubes, numbers 2, 3, 4, and 5; star tubes, numbers 27 and 30; flower tube, number 104; and flower nail, number 7.

For greater convenience standard metal tube numbers will be used in reference to size of cone openings. If you are using paper cones exclusively, translate No. 2 as two thirty-seconds of an inch (or one-sixteenth); No. 3 as three thirty-seconds of an inch; No. 4 as four thirty-seconds of an inch (or one-eighth); No. 5 as five thirty-seconds of an inch. Although this system is not strictly accurate, it will do very well for all practical purposes.

Some decorators, especially those who are working on many cakes professionally, use large canvas, rubber, or plastic bags so that they do not have to stop for refills so often. They usually use paper cones for more delicate work, however. The large bags may be purchased at a bakers' wholesale supply house, or they may be made at home.

The proper metal tube is dropped into the bag, the bag is filled with icing, the top of the bag is closed by grasping it with the left hand, and pressure is exerted near the bottom of the bag by grasping it with the right hand. This way of exerting pressure requires more skill and experience, as well as strength, in order to secure even and controlled results. It is not recommended for the beginner.

The metal ornamenting syringe is not used to any extent by the professional decorator because the nature of the mechanism renders pressure control difficult. The resulting work tends to be wavy, irregular, and amateurish in appearance.

Metal syringes and canvas, rubber or plastic bags also have to be washed frequently, which is a decided disadvantage. The

---

*If you have difficulty buying tubes and other decorating equipment and materials, you may obtain further information by addressing the Snyder School of Cake Decoration, 16841 Grand River Ave., Detroit 27, Michigan.

inexpensive paper cones serve very well and can be destroyed.

On pp. 15 ff. you have learned how to use paper cones alone or with metal tubes. Now it is time to use some bottles of vegetable coloring.

COLORING ICING

Place 1 cup of icing in the center of a dinner plate or pie tin.

Place a tablespoon of icing near the edge of the same plate.

Shake a few drops of red vegetable coloring on the small portion.

Blend the red color evenly through the small portion with a table knife.

Take a part of the red-colored icing and blend it evenly through the large portion of icing on the same plate.

Add more of bright-colored icing as necessary to color large portion a pastel pink.

❊   ❊   ❊

Place ½ cup icing in the center of a second plate.

Place 1 tablespoon of icing near the edge of the same plate.

Shake a few drops of green and one or two drops of yellow vegetable coloring on the small portion.

Blend the colors evenly through small portion with a second table knife.

Take a part of the green-colored icing and blend it evenly through the large portion of icing on the same plate.

Add more of bright-colored icing as necessary to obtain a shade of pastel of yellow-green that will match the pastel pink.

❊   ❊   ❊

Spread a thin layer of white icing on the back of a cake pan, pie tin, or cookie pan.

Close storage container so that rest of icing will keep smooth indefinitely.

Notes: The liquid vegetable-color kits may be purchased in any large grocery store. They contain a very helpful color chart.

Black, Christmas red, and certain other shades can be obtained only in paste or powdered form. They can be bought in wholesale supply houses.

The method of coloring as outlined above makes it possible to obtain exactly the desired shade.

Whenever you are making a green that is to be used for stems and leaves, add a drop or two of yellow. This will give you a yellow-green that is characteristic of living plants.

Use the colors and shades which will please the recipient of the cake. The small child, for instance, usually likes bright colors and lots of them. An elderly person is apt to prefer fewer colors, lighter shades, and greater use of white decoration. Of course, Christmas cakes and the like demand bright colors. However, the safest rule where food decoration is concerned might be: When in doubt, use pastel shades. Most people find them more appetizing.

If any portion of the icing is too stiff, just add a few drops of water. If the same icing is used over and over again for practice work, add a little shortening to it to keep it from becoming dry and hard to manage.

When an actual cake is being iced, it is best to use one of your regular frostings. Keep decorating icing on hand primarily for decorating.

By now you must be impatient to fill those cones.

FILLING AND FOLDING CONES

If you are using metal tubes with paper cones, you may use one of two methods, depending upon which seems to work best for you.

The first method is to cut off the point of the paper cone so that the opening is a little larger than the metal-tube opening.

Drop the metal tube into the paper cone so that the metal-tube opening projects beyond the paper.

Then fill the cone with icing as demonstrated in Figures 5, 6 and 7A,B,C,D, and pp. 22 ff.

✿   ✿   ✿

Figure 5

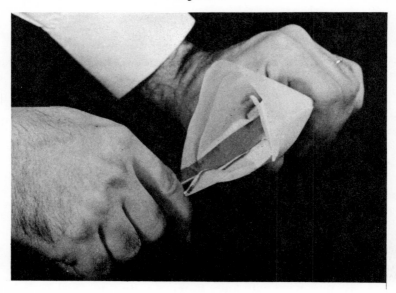

Figure 6

Figure 7

The second method requires two paper cones.

Fill first cone as demonstrated in Figures 5, 6 and 7A,B,C, and described in this section.

Then cut an opening that is a little larger than the metal-tube opening.

Place metal tube over paper-cone opening.

Cut second paper-cone opening about the same size as the first one.

Have metal tube of first cone pointed up.

Put second paper cone over metal tube so that second cone holds metal tube in place against outside of first cone. (Fig. 7E.)

This second method is best when you are first beginning to learn, or when the paper is of poor quality.

✿　　✿　　✿

Here is the best way to fill a cone with icing, whether or not you are using metal tubes.

Mix pink icing with knife to remove crustiness and air bubbles that form when icing is exposed to the air.

Place paper cone in left hand so that the *inside* loose edge of paper is on the bottom, just above the thumb. (The inside loose edge of paper is marked with pencil in Fig. 5.)

With icing on *lower* side of knife, place knife inside cone as far as it will go. (Fig. 5.)

Move left thumb toward cone's large opening.

Press knife against paper and left thumb.

Continuing the pressure, withdraw knife and leave icing in the cone. (Fig. 6.)

Repeat until the cone is two-thirds full.

Hold cone point down, with both hands at top.

Flatten paper at top with both thumbs until icing reaches point of cone. (Fig. 7A.)

Fold top corners and sides part way toward center with thumbs. (Fig. 7B.)

Fold top down as you would a partially emptied toothpaste tube. (Fig. 7C.)

Fill a second paper cone with green icing in a similar manner.

Notes: This method of folding keeps the icing from coming out of the top at awkward moments.

Always mix icing again just before placing it in a cone. This will keep crustiness and air bubbles from interfering with your work.

When you are using the *double*-cone system (p. 23), cut the first cone enough so that the bottom third of the metal tube will contain no paper when it is placed on the first cone. The icing will flow more freely and will respond more accurately to pressure.

Some interesting and beautiful effects can be obtained by variegating colors in the same cone of icing. Flowers, edgings, writing, and figure piping can be made in this way.

Carefully place white icing along one side of paper cone, increasing the amount as the cone becomes wider.

Turn the cone around and carefully place some colored

icing on the side opposite the white icing, increasing the amount as the cone becomes wider.

Close the cone in the usual manner. (Fig. 7.)

Turn cone or metal tube so that color comes out on top, side, or bottom of decoration, as you wish—as soon as you exert pressure on the cone.

Try filling the cone with two different shades of the same color. When making stems and leaves, use a small amount of brown icing with the green icing.

Dip a small brush into full-strength or diluted liquid vegetable coloring; draw one or more streaks of color along the *inside* length of cone; then being careful not to disturb color, add white or pastel-colored icing.

Let's see what we can do with these cones of icing. As you practice the following techniques, remember that you are going to use every one of them on the first cake you decorate.

II

Decorating the First Cake

If you are using metal tubes, use a No. 2 tube, according to directions on pp. 21 ff. If you are using a plain paper cone proceed as follows: With a pair of sharp scissors cut off the point of the green cone squarely so that the opening is a true circle, one-sixteenth inch in diameter. Use a ruler to guide you.

Grasp the cone in such manner that the folded cushion of paper is vertical and smooth on the right side.

The paper cushion should be pressed against the cushion of muscle just below the thumb.

One or two fingers should press against the top of the cone; the other fingers should press against the bottom of the cone.

Most of the pressure should be exerted against the paper cushion by the cushion of muscle just below the thumb. (Notice hand position in Fig. 13 on p. 39.)

When the cone is almost empty, or when you are using a very small cone, press the thumb itself against the paper cushion. (See Fig. 14C on p. 40.)

Grasping the cone in the proper manner, exert pressure. If

the icing does not come through the opening easily at the slightest pressure, clip a half-inch off the cone, and squeeze the icing out of the cone and back on the plate. Thin the icing with some water and fill another cone with the softer mixture.

If you are using the double-cone system with a metal tube, be certain that the opening of the first cone is cut large enough before the metal tube is placed over it.

When the icing comes through the opening easily, you are ready to practice.

✿   ✿   ✿

Hold the cone at a 45-degree angle and tilt the cone to the right. (Fig. 8B.)

Just barely touching the point to the white-iced pan, make a row of elongated S-shaped stems, about one and one-half inches long and two inches apart. (Fig. 8A.)

Bring the cone toward you as you work.

Lower cone to white icing slightly as you finish bottom of stem.

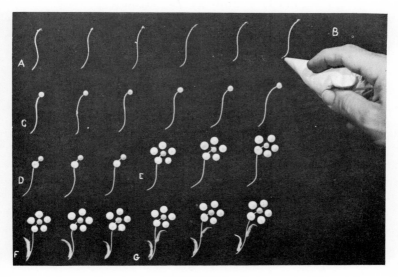

Figure 8

Release pressure.
Then lift cone.

*   *   *

Holding the cone perpendicularly, touch the top of first stem with the point of the cone.

Press out a green flower center about one-eighth inch in diameter.

Release pressure.

Then lift cone.

Put green centers on rest of stems in a similar fashion. (Fig. 8C.)

*   *   *

If you are using metal tubes, use a No. 4 tube, according to directions on pp. 21 ff. If you are using a plain paper cone, proceed as follows: With a pair of sharp scissors cut off the point of the pink cone squarely so that the opening is a true circle, one-eighth inch in diameter. Use a ruler to guide you.

Grasp the cone in the proper manner and exert pressure. If the icing does not flow easily at the slightest pressure, thin it down before continuing. If you are using a double-cone system with a metal tube, be certain that no paper is clogging the metal-tube opening.

If the icing flows easily you are ready to practice.

*   *   *

Holding the pink cone perpendicularly, touch the stem just below the green flower center.

Press out a pink flower petal about three-sixteenths inch in diameter. (Fig. 8D.)

Release pressure.

Then lift cone.

Space four more similar petals around center.

Practice on rest of flowers, spacing five petals evenly around each green center.

Leave a slight space between petals and center, and between the petals themselves. (Fig. 8E.)

*   *   *

Holding green cone perpendicular to surface, place it at base of stem.

Tilt cone to left.

Barely touching the surface, press out a flat, narrow leaf as you lead cone along curve of stem and then branch away from stem to the left. (Fig. 8F.)

Tilting cone to right, place a second leaf higher up, on opposite side of same stem. (Fig. 8G.)

Release pressure gradually as you finish so that each leaf is pointed.

Notes: Place leaf in the "hollow" of a stem's curve for most graceful results.

Vary length and width of leaves on same stem for a more pleasing effect. Vary the angles at which leaves on same stem branch away.

For whom are you going to decorate your first cake?

Cut a circle of cardboard the same size as the top of the cake you are going to decorate.

Take a pencil and write the message you are going to use. Be careful to center it properly, leaving a one-and-one-half-inch margin all around the edge for flowers and edgings. Use an eraser as often as you need it.

If you have trouble forming your letters properly, refer to the model alphabets in Figure 9A.

When the message is written and centered properly, retrace it until it is very dark and legible.

Place a sheet of transparent waxed paper on top of the cardboard and fasten it with paper clips or thumb tacks.

❄   ❄   ❄

Make a No. 2 cone of pink icing. The icing must be very soft.

Hold the pink cone at a 45-degree angle.

Tilt the cone to the right. (Fig. 9A.)

Figure 9

Just barely touching the surface, keep a steady pressure while tracing over the letters. Rest every two or three letters at first until you become used to sustaining pressure.

Practice with a No. 3 cone and with a No. 4 cone. You will find that it is more difficult to write with a larger cone opening. However, with study and practice larger tube writing can be accomplished successfully.

Since the icing is thicker than ink or graphite, you may find it piling up and toppling over (especially with larger cone openings) wherever a letter is formed by retracing a part of it.

An example is the written letter *a*. Notice that the tail of that letter goes down the top right side of the original loop. (Fig. 9B.)

To avoid the toppling effect or sprawling effect, thin the top right side of the original loop by pushing the cone against the surface lightly. (Fig. 9C.)

Then, holding the cone in the original position, finish making the tail of the letter.

As a general rule thin any part of a written letter that is going to be retraced.

✿   ✿   ✿

Another way to avoid the sprawling effect is to omit any retracing. This can be done in the following manner:

Make the original loop of the written *a* the same thickness throughout.

Stop pressure and lift the cone when it reaches the top of the original loop.

Place the cone part way down the right side of the original loop.

Start pressure and finish the letter. (Fig. 9D.)

When you have finished tracing the letters in your message, scrape the icing off the waxed paper with a table knife and continue practicing until your writing is satisfactory.

MAKING EDGINGS AND SIDE DESIGNS

Fill a paper cone with soft white icing. Use a No. 5 metal tube or cut the paper cone so that the opening is about five thirty-seconds of an inch in diameter.

Turn a deep metal sauce pan or an angel-food cake pan upside down and pretend that it is a cake.

Hold the white cone perpendicular to the top edge, and about one-sixteenth inch away from the pan.

Press steadily and hold cone still until a three-eighths-inch disc is formed.

Release pressure.

Then lift cone.

Repeat around top edge of pan, making all the discs the same size and thickness and spacing them about one-sixteenth inch apart. (Fig. 10A.)

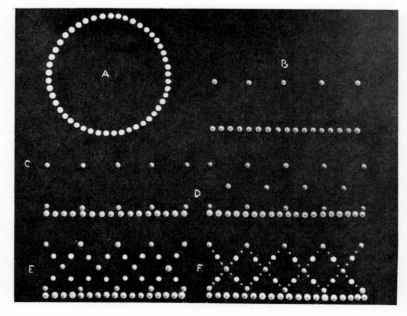

Figure 10

Use a No. 5 metal tube with a cone of soft pink icing, or cut a paper cone so that the opening is about five thirty-seconds inch in diameter.

Hold the pink cone at right angles to the bottom edge of the pan.

Using the same technique as for the top, space pink discs evenly around the bottom edge. (Fig. 10B, lower part.)

Using the same pink cone, space eight small pink dots at equal intervals around the side of the pan near the top. (Fig. 10B, upper part.)

Space eight small pink dots at equal intervals around the side near the bottom, directly below pink dots at top. (Fig. 10C.)

Place another row of eight pink dots around the side, in the middle section, mismatching them with dots at top and bottom. (Fig. 10D.)

Place white dots between pink dots in such a way that it results in a latticed effect. (Fig. 10E.)

Place small dots of green between white and pink dots, and the latticed effect is more pronounced. (Fig. 10F.)

ICING THE CAKE

Make a layer cake and ice it smoothly with a regular white icing. Here are some suggestions that may help you.

Allow the layers to cool for an hour or more before applying frosting. If all the steam is out of the cake, it is less likely to break when it is being handled.

Have icing soft enough so that it will spread easily and smoothly. Icing that is too dry and heavy will tear the cake.

Cut a piece of cardboard the same size as the cake and place the first layer on the cardboard. This will make it possible to move the cake without breaking it.

If the layer is high in the middle, take a French knife or some other sharp knife and slice off the "hump." This will keep the second layer from cracking through the center.

As soon as the first layer is level, spread jam, icing, or other filling over the top.

Place the second layer on top of the first one. If the second layer is high in the center, and if the cake is to be two layers only, place the second layer so that the rounded part is on top. If you want the top absolutely level, trim the second layer with a French knife and turn the layer upside down before placing it on top of the first one. You will have less trouble icing the top of the cake if the cut side is in the middle.

If the cake is to be three layers, be careful to have the bottom two layers level before icing between them and placing the third layer on top. Otherwise the top layer may crack through the center after the cake has been standing for a certain time.

If layers are thinner at one edge than they are at the other, turn layers so that cake will finally be level.

If you have a Lazy Susan or a turntable of some kind, you will find that it is much easier to ice the top and sides smoothly. Metal turntables can be purchased at a bakers' wholesale supply house. (Fig. 11.)

Figure 11

This device speeds up certain types of decorating work also. It is not absolutely necessary, but it is a decided help.

If cake tends to be crumbly, refrigerate it until it is hard before applying icing.

Place cake on turntable. With a spatula pointed downward place portions of icing at intervals around the sides. Make no attempt to smooth each portion, or you will put crumbs in the icing. (If you do have icing that is full of crumbs, use it between layers.)

Then point the spatula downward in vertical position at the left side of the cake. Press right edge of the spatula lightly against the left side of the cake and with the left hand turn the cake to the left. Stop as necessary to remove excess icing from the knife.

Put considerable icing on top of cake. Too little icing will cause it to crumb excessively. Turn cake against horizontal spatula and remove excess icing. Alternately work spatula at the side of the cake and on top.

Put spatula at 45-degree angle and just barely touch it to top edge of cake as it is turned slowly. Remove final bit of excess icing in this way.

Dip spatula in hot water. Shake off excess water. Turn sides and top of cake against hot, wet blade several times until icing is very smooth and shiny. Dip knife in hot water frequently. Allow icing to dry before decorating cake.

Cut a cardboard circle that is three or four inches greater in diameter than the cake. Fasten a paper doily or parts of several doilies (see Fig. 44, p. 95) to cardboard with stapler or icing. Cut wax-paper circle that is one inch larger in diameter than the cake. Fasten it to doilies and cardboard with stapler or icing.

Put spatula under cardboard that is under cake. Lift and move edge of cake just beyond edge of turntable. With both hands lift cake from turntable and place it in center of wax-paper circle.

Wait until the icing is no longer sticky before starting to decorate. If you are in a hurry, put the cake in the refrigerator for a few minutes.

If you do not like to bake, stop at your favorite bakery and buy a cake that is iced and ready for decoration.

DECORATING THE FIRST CAKE

Place the edge of a straight knife very lightly against the icing where you intend to write. These faint marks will help you to write in straight lines. (Refer to Fig. 12 as necessary.)

Figure 12

Take a toothpick and sketch lightly into the icing the inscription which you practiced previously. Be careful to keep a one-and-one-half-inch margin around the cake top.

When you are sure that your spacing is correct, write the inscription with pink icing, using a cone with a one-eighth-inch opening or a No. 4 metal tube.

If you make a mistake, just take a table knife and carefully remove the pink icing and start over again.

Trace over the pink writing with green icing from a one-sixteenth-inch cone opening or a No. 2 metal tube.

Take a small metal paper clip or similar piece of wire and bend it into the shape of an elongated, flattened-out letter S one and one-half inches long, with a handle sticking upright at each end.

Holding the wire device parallel with the edge of the cake, press it into the icing lightly at eight evenly spaced intervals around the cake top. If the wire becomes sticky, dip it in water or corn starch before continuing. Go around the cake in a clockwise fashion, always pointing the wire device in the same direction.

Using a green cone with one-sixteenth-inch opening or a No. 2 metal tube, fill in stems.

Starting at the stem nearest you, put a flower at the left end of the stem.

Turn the cake so that another stem is directly in front of you. Put a flower at the left end of the second stem.

Continue until there is a flower on each stem, all pointing clockwise.

Put green leaves on each stem.

Put white discs on top, near edge of cake.

Put pink discs around side of cake, near bottom edge.

Place pink, white, and green decorations on side of cake.

You are now a cake decorator. But this is only the first in a long list of successful cakes to come.

III

More Flowers, Leaves, Stems

MORE FLOWERS

You have learned how to make a flower with a plain tube or round paper-cone opening. For the sake of variety, use any star tube you happen to have. Use a No. 27 star tube if you have that size. The flowers we are about to make can also be made with a plain tube.

When you use a star tube, keep it at right angles to the surface. Then the stars will be even on all sides.

Touch the star tube to the surface. Keep the tube at right angles to the surface. Notice cone position in Figure 13.

Press cone until a star is completely formed.

Release pressure.

Then lift cone straight up from the surface.

If the star is not shaped properly, check the paper cone inside the metal tube when you are using the double-cone system. The inner cone of paper must be cut short enough or it will clog small openings of star tube. (Figs. 13A,B.)

If the star tube is not clogged with paper, check metal points of star tube to be sure that they are opened evenly. The metal is soft and easily bent.

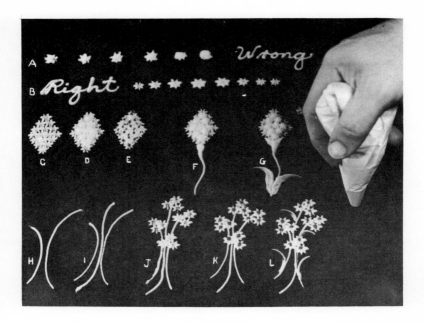

Figure 13

The next flower is formed by placing stars (white or colored) in rows: top row, 1 star; row two, 2 stars; row three, 3 stars; row four, 4 stars; row five, 3 stars; row six, 2 stars. (Fig. 13C.) Crowd the center rows a little bit and the flower will be more rounded. Put two in every row and a single star on top of each row, and the flower will resemble a hyacinth.

Place a second layer of stars on top of the others: row two, 1 star; row three, 2 stars; row four, 3 stars; row five, 2 stars; row six, 1 star. (Fig. 13D.)

If you wish, put a dot of different colored icing in the center of each star. (Fig. 13E.)

Using No. 3 green cone, form heavy green base to flower and bring cone downward to form graceful stem. (Fig. 13F.)

Using more pressure make leaves somewhat larger than the ones on your first decorated cake. (Fig. 13G.)

✻   ✻   ✻

Another flower can be made in the following manner:

First, curve two stems of different length against each other so that their backs almost touch. (Fig. 13H.)

Draw a longer stem in S-fashion between first two stems. (Fig. 13I.)

Put three stars (white or colored) at top of each stem. (Fig. 13J.) Put another group of three stars in lower middle of stem arrangement.

Put dots of contrasting icing in centers of stars. (Fig. 13K.)

Draw thin leaves along stems at several points. (Fig. 13L.)

❊ ❊ ❊

For still other varieties of flowers which stand away from the surface more, cut a very small paper cone of icing as follows:

Flatten point of cone between thumb and index finger. (Fig. 14A.)

With sharp scissors cut a diagonal line about one-eighth inch across. (Fig. 14B.)

Hold paper flower cone so the longest part is touching the

Figure 14

cake. The shortest part is upright. The cone is held at a 45-degree angle.

Press out an upright petal. (Fig. 14C.)

Release pressure and lift cone toward you.

Put base of cone in same position as before, but point cone to the right of the first petal.

Press out second petal, release pressure, and lift cone toward you. (Fig. 14D.) The result is a pair of petals in V-formation.

Make three stems as in Figures 13H,I.

Place pairs of flower petals on stems, alternating from left to right on the way down each stem. (Figs. 14E,F.)

Place stem tube at base of each flower.

Press out small leaf against lower third of each flower. (Fig. 14G.)

Add small thin leaves directly to stems also. (Fig. 14H.)

These imaginative flowers should stimulate you to invent different arrangements and combinations of your own.

MORE LEAVES

A wider type of leaf than the one made previously is best formed by a very small paper cone that has been cut in a V-shape after it has been filled with *soft* icing. The paper cone should be made of a triangle that is no longer than six inches on each of its two equal sides. The filled paper cone is cut in the following manner:

Press point of cone flat between thumb and index finger. (Fig. 15A.)

With the left hand hold the cone point downward. Cut a left diagonal one-fourth inch long. (Fig. 15B.)

Turn cone over so that diagonal points downward and to the right. (Fig. 15C.)

Cut second left diagonal so that V is formed. (Fig. 15D.)

Make an S-shaped stem with a stem tube.

Press some icing out of leaf cone against a practice surface. As you gradually release pressure, slowly lift cone until the icing breaks away from the cone. Notice the little point of icing that projects beyond the point of the cone.

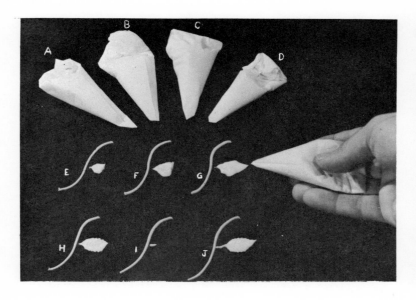

Figure 15

Place leaf cone in cupped palm of hand so that pressure is exerted with the end of thumb. The V-opening of the cone should be parallel with the palm. (Fig. 15G.)

Place point of icing one-eighth inch from stem. Hold the cone at an angle approximately 45-degrees to the surface.

Start pressure slowly and move away from the stem at the same time. (Fig. 15E.)

As cone is pulled away from stem, gradually increase pressure for a short distance. (Fig. 15F.)

And then gradually reduce pressure to nothing, as the cone comes to the end of the leaf. (Fig. 15G.)

If you wish to make leaves with ridges in them, add slight backward and forward motions to the movement and pressure already described. (Fig. 15H.)

Each leaf is actually attached by a very small stem to the large stem. A slight separation of leaf and main stem will cause such an illusion.

If you prefer, insert a small, short stem before making leaf. (Figs. 15I,J.)

Use this wide type of leaf made with the V-shaped cone in the previous flower arrangements. Notice how different the flowers appear when you give them different leaves.

If you have difficulty making the leaves come to a point, thin the icing more or cut the paper cone so that the V is wider and less sharply pointed.

POINSETTIAS

Poinsettias are also made with the V-cut paper cone. When you put them on a cake, use a bright Christmas red icing for the petals and a Christmas green for the stems and leaves. When you practice, you can use white or any color that is handy.

Make three-inch flattened-out S-stems with a No. 3 green cone. (Fig. 16A.)

Place a green disc, one-fourth inch in diameter, at top of each stem. (Fig. 16B.)

Using a No. 2 yellow cone, place several small dots on top of green discs. (Fig. 16C.)

Using a small camel's-hair brush, touch the yellow dots very lightly with red vegetable coloring. (Fig. 16D.)

Cut a one-fourth-inch red V-cone. (Figs. 15A,B,C,D.)

Make seven or more leaf-like petals so that they almost touch the center and do not touch each other. (Fig. 16H.)

Shape each one differently. (Fig. 16E.)

Make each a different length. (Fig. 16F.)

Have them come away from the center at different angles. (Fig. 16G.)

Cut a one-fourth-inch green V-cone.

Almost touch stem as you place large leaves on either side. (Fig. 16I.)

LILIES OF THE VALLEY

Lilies of the Valley may be portrayed with or without leaves. If leaves are used, the paper cone should be cut so that the widest part of the V is three-eighths of an inch.

The leaf starts small at the base, becoming much larger

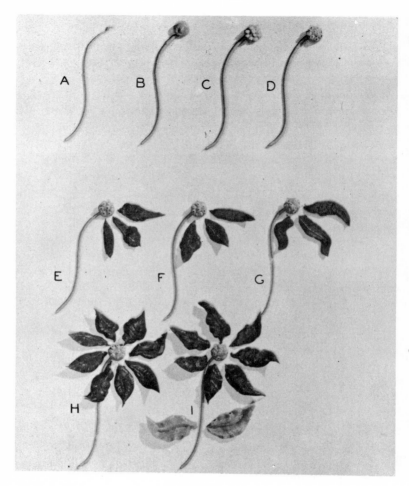

Figure 16

as it comes upward, and then tapering to a point. (Fig. 17A.)

Vary the length and formation of leaves for best effect. (Fig. 17B.)

Drop green stems from No. 2 cone against background of leaves or by themselves. (Figs. 17C,D.) (See pp. 53 f. for instruction in drop technique.)

Using a No. 3 cone of very soft white icing, and keeping the point of the cone in the icing, curve a short, fat, carrot-shaped bit of icing slightly to the left as you bring the cone toward you. (Fig. 17E.)

Overlapping the first "carrot" of icing, place a similar "carrot" of icing to the right of the first one, curving it slightly to the right. (Fig. 17F.)

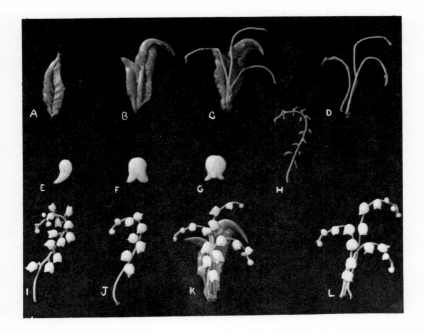

Place another "carrot" of icing on top of the first two, tilting the point slightly upward. (Fig. 17G.)

The white icing for the lilies should be so soft that the individual "carrots" lose their individuality and become one flower. Keep points of "carrots" very short.

Using a No. 2 cone of green icing, attach very short stems to the main stems. (Fig. 17H.)

Place lilies on small stems so that most of them hang down-

ward like bells. The blossoms become smaller toward the top of
the main stems. (Fig. 17I.)

Some decorators attach lilies directly to the main stem,
omitting the very short stems. (Fig. 17J.)

Figures 17K and 17L show arrangements with and without
leaves.

USING A FLOWER NAIL

Certain flowers have to be made with a flower nail. Others
can be made more easily with this very simple tool.

If you have bought one, you will notice that it is merely a
metal disc soldered to a nail. If you have not bought one, you
can pound a nail through a bottle cap and seal it together with
some tape. This will do temporarily.

Keep arms low and close to your body as you make nail
flowers. This position steadies both hands.

If you are left-handed, please remember to reverse as necessary the directions which follow.

Press flower nail in left hand between the end of the thumb
and the center of the first two fingers. (Fig. 18.)

Turn the nail by moving thumb toward the ends of the
fingers. Ordinarily the icing is put on the nail during this cycle.

Move thumb back to original position. *No* icing goes on the
nail during this cycle.

Hold arms close to your sides and keep the nail low and the
disc level.

APPLE BLOSSOMS

The paper flower cone that was cut once diagonally (see
p. 40, Fig. 14) can be used for making miniature apple blossoms, roses, etc. If the paper cone is cut much larger, however,
the flower petals become shapeless because the paper will bulge
out of shape. Therefore, when you wish to make larger flowers
of this type, it becomes necessary to use a metal wedge-shaped,
No. 104 flower tube. It is also necessary to use a stiffer icing so
that the petals will keep their shape. Just sift more powdered

Figure 18

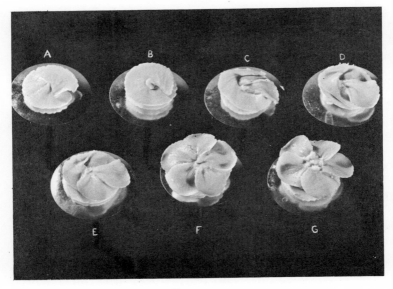

Figure 19

sugar into your icing until it is of the appropriate consistency.

Make up a *variegated* No. 104 cone of icing. (See pp. 20 f.) Use white and delicate pink icing. Turn metal tube so that pink icing comes out of the large end, which is always nearest nail or cake.

Place bottom (large part) of flower tube against top center of disc. Have cone almost level with disc. Tip top (small part) of flower tube to right so that it is almost level with disc.

Press out icing and turn nail once around at the same time. (Fig. 19A.)

Lift cone straight up one-sixteenth inch and turn nail around a second time as icing is pressed out. (Fig. 19B.)

This makes a spiral platform that will make it possible for us to remove the apple blossom after it is made.

Put bottom edge of flower tube at center of spiral platform. Have cone almost level with disc. Tip top of tube to right so that it makes a 30-degree angle with the disc. (See Fig. 18 for tube position.)

Using a gradually increasing pressure on the icing bring the tube a distance of one-sixteenth of an inch from the center and toward the edge of the spiral platform of icing (Fig. 19C) as the nail is being turned.

Continuing the turning of the nail, and gradually reducing the pressure bring the tube straight back to the starting point at the center. (Fig. 19D.)

Start the second petal just under the right side of the first one. (Fig. 19E.)

Continue until five petals are spaced evenly about the center. (Fig. 19F.)

Place table knife under spiral platform of icing, turn nail, and remove flower.

Place flower on cake or pan by pushing flower from knife with end of flower nail.

Put several pale yellow dots in center of blossom. (Fig. 19G.)

Violets, orange blossoms, pansies, and many other flowers are made in a similar way. A little study of real flowers and good pictures will help you to get the proportions and colors right.

In order to make nail roses properly it is usually necessary to thicken the icing by sifting more powdered sugar into it. When the petals hold their shape the icing is thick enough.

See p. 46 and Figure 18 for instruction in the use of a flower nail.

Put a flower nail in the left hand and a No. 104 cone of thickened icing in the right hand.

Tilt metal tube to left so that base (large part of wedge) is just touching disc and the top is directly over the center of the nail. Keeping the same position, exert heavy pressure on the icing and turn the nail once or twice until a solid cone is formed. (Fig. 20A.)

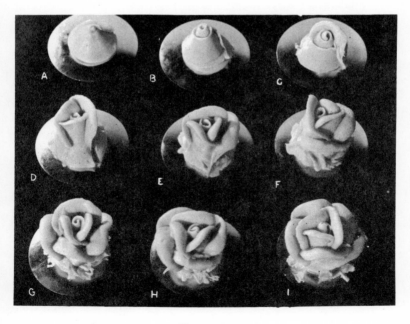

Figure 20

Place flower tube in vertical position with base of tube in top of cone. Using light pressure on icing, turn the nail two or three times while bringing base of tube straight down to the metal disc. This will form a spiral of icing. If spiral is too open, tilt top of tube downward. (Fig. 20B.)

Keeping tube in vertical position with base touching disc and center of spiral, turn nail, press icing, and lift tube straight up (just above top of spiral) and straight down to disc. This petal should go half-way around spiral center. Keep base of tube pushed into center of rose when making this and other petals. (Fig. 20C.)

Start second center petal one-third of the way back of first petal so the petals will overlap. Make second petal half-way around center.

Overlapping second petal by one-third, make third petal half-way around center. (Fig. 20D.)

The three center petals are a little higher than the spiral. The outside petals which we are about to make are a little lower than the three center petals.

Tilt top of flower tube to the right, more or less, depending upon how open the rose is to be. Place base of tube at disc and against the flower. Turn nail, press icing, and move tube up and to the right in a straight line, and then back to nail. (Fig. 20E.)

This petal and the rest of the outside petals are brought a third of the way around, each one overlapping the preceding petal by a third of the width of the petal. All outside petals are lower than center petals. (Figs. 20F,G,H,I.)

Just before the rose is removed from the nail, trim the bottom of the rose by cutting at the sides with a table knife as the nail is turned slowly. Then place the knife under the rose, turn the nail and remove the rose. Push rose off knife with point of flower nail.

Figure 21 shows some typical errors in rose making.

If the cone has a large hole in the middle, keep top of tube over exact center of disc until cone is completed. (Fig. 21A.) Make a large cone with a star tube if you have too much diffi-

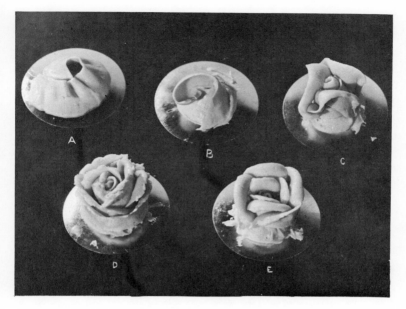

Figure 21

culty in making it with a flower tube. Then wrap a No. 104 ribbon of icing around it.

If the spiral falls down the other side of the cone (Fig. 21B), be sure to put base of tube into top center of icing cone before turning nail. Use small amount of pressure and turn nail just as soon as you press icing.

If the petals lose shape, be careful to press base of tube against center of flower until petals are complete. (Fig. 21C.)

If the petals tear at the edges, increase pressure when the nail is being turned. (Fig. 21D.) Never tilt top of tube to left if you are turning nail according to directions on p. 50. Double-check size of inner-cone opening if you are using double-cone system. The last third of the metal tube must contain no paper. Be sure that the wedge-shaped opening of the flower tube is not pinched together at the top.

If the rose appears flat or sunken, be careful to build cone and spiral high enough. (Fig. 21E.) Add a second spiral if necessary. Tube must be moved up and down while center and outside petals are being formed. Make' sure that outside petals do not come as high as center petals.

❀   ❀   ❀

Each rose opens differently. As soon as you have mastered the basic elements try imitating real roses or good pictures of them. In this way you will become versatile. Here in Figure 22 are some variations on the basic rose.

Make cone, spiral and two or three center petals. Trim base of rosebud so that it rounds properly. (Fig. 22A.) Tilt top of tube to right when making petals if you want roses to open more.

Make cone, spiral and a second spiral for greater height. (Fig. 22B.)

Using a double spiral, make a large rose. (Fig. 22C.)

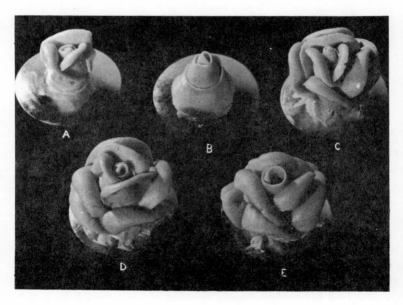

Figure 22

Make large rose with center petals straight and high, and outside petals low and opening to the right. (Fig. 22D.)

Make large soft rose with open spiral, diagonal center petals, and nearly horizontal outside petals. (Fig. 22E.)

Notes: These individual flowers or small groups of flowers which you have just practiced are excellent for cake squares, cupcakes, cookies and petit fours. In some cases smaller tubes or smaller paper-cone openings will have to be used.

Try these new flowers and leaves on the tops or sides of large cakes also.

A first-hand study of real flowers will repay the student a thousand-fold. Nature is the best teacher. If you don't grow the particular flowers you want, or if it isn't the right season of the year for growing them, patronize a florist shop.

It is also a good idea to observe bakery windows, magazines, newspapers, greeting cards, wallpaper, rugs and any other objects that show good design. Study flower books in the public library. Buy ten-cent books about flowers in the dime store. Study seed catalogues.

Buy an inexpensive, accordion-type, cardboard file at an office-supply store. Under appropriate headings such as "Birthday," "Shower," "Wedding," "Flowers," "Designs," "Christmas," and many others, file clippings, ideas, sketches, and any cardboard or wire devices you may have used for previous cakes. Such a file will stimulate your imagination and bring about a refreshing and endless variety of decorations.

DROP TECHNIQUE

Until now you have used a drawing technique in making stems; that is, one side of cone or tube opening was touching the surface lightly as you drew the stem. On very soft, sticky or uneven surfaces it is necessary to drop the stems into place. Therefore, it is good to know the drop technique as well as the drawing technique.

Some decorators always use the drop technique for long straight lines or long curved stem lines because they find it easier to form smooth, even lines. It is especially recommended for beginners who find it difficult to draw stems gracefully. The drop technique begins as follows:

With a No. 3 cone of very soft green icing start just enough pressure to fasten icing to surface. Too much pressure will leave an ugly mound of icing at the beginning of the stem. (Fig. 23A.)

If icing isn't fastened to surface, a hook may be formed. (Fig. 23B.)

After fastening icing properly, continue a steady pressure and slowly lift cone one inch straight up from surface. Continuing a steady pressure, make straight lines and curved lines by keeping the point of the cone one-quarter inch ahead of the vertical column of icing. Bring the lines toward you for best control. (Figs. 23C,D.)

Figure 23E represents a *wrong* method for taking off from the surface; it resembles a standard jet plane take-off. The icing becomes too thin or it breaks.

Figure 23F represents the *right* method; it might be called the helicopter technique. First, fasten the icing to the surface. Then lift the cone one inch straight up.

Letting the column of icing fall almost vertically as the cone travels in a curved or straight line, there is no thinning or breaking of icing. (Fig. 23G.)

If the column of icing gets ahead of the cone, the line becomes irregular or full of loops. (Fig. 23H.)

Release pressure just before the cone descends toward the surface in order to avoid loop at the end of a line. (Fig. 23I.)

For a smooth line keep the point of the cone one-quarter inch *ahead* of the column of icing.

Always bring the lines toward you for best control.

STEMS

Using "helicopter" or drop technique, start at center of surface and bring stem to the left and toward you in a smooth curve. (Fig. 23J.)

Make two more stems in a similar manner. Turn surface before making each stem so that cone can be brought toward

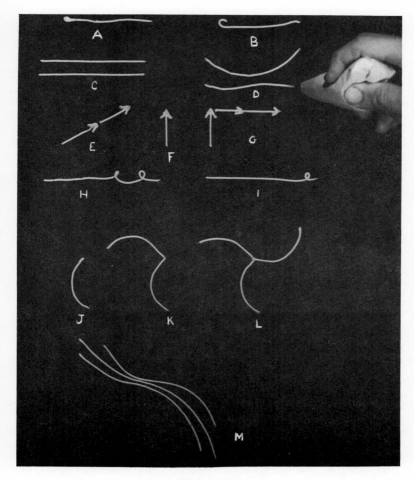

Figure 23

you each time. These stems will be used for formal corsage in Chapter IV. (Figs. 23K,L.)

Using drop technique, make three elongated S-curves so that they come near each other at a central point. (Fig. 23M.)

Always turn the surface so that cone can be brought toward you. These stems will be used for informal corsage in Chapter IV.

LATTICING

The latticing technique resembles drop technique. There are certain differences, however. The tube is not kept so high above the surface. The column of icing is pulled toward you slightly so that it is diagonal rather than vertical.

If the icing is pulled too much, it breaks. If the icing is not pulled enough, the lines will not be absolutely straight when they hit the surface. It requires a great deal of practice to perfect a happy medium.

When you are latticing, start at the center of the pattern with a diagonal line. (Fig. 24A.)

Make rest of diagonals to the right and to the left of the original. (Fig. 24B.)

Place a center diagonal going in opposite direction and at right angles to first layer of diagonals. (Fig. 24C.)

Fill in rest of diagonals to left and right. Edge latticing with bead work. (Fig. 24D.)

See p. 80 and Figure 37H for instruction in bead work.

If a third layer of latticing is used, place it directly above the first layer. A fourth layer would be placed above the second layer.

Latticing is used in Figures 44 and 45. (See pp. 95 f.)

In the next chapter we shall explore various ways in which flowers can be arranged attractively.

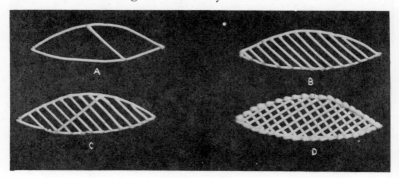

Figure 24

IV

Flower Arrangements

CORSAGE ARRANGEMENT

Flower-arrangement techniques are basically the same for all flowers, however small, large, simple or complicated they may be.

In this formal corsage arrangement notice the repetition in the design. (Fig. 25A.) Countless variations will suggest themselves. A formal style can be placed at the center of a cake top, with or without an inscription. For the small flowers in this illustration use No. 104 flower tube and the same method that is demonstrated on pp. 40 f. and in Figure 14.

An informal corsage arrangement is always interesting because its construction is subtle. (Fig. 25B.) Notice, for instance, that the small flowers at the extreme right tend to form an elongated S-curve with the small flowers at the extreme lower left.

Balancing this style of corsage against an inscription calls for ingenuity. If one is not careful, the flowers are on one half of the cake and the writing is on the other half—a result which destroys the appearance of informality.

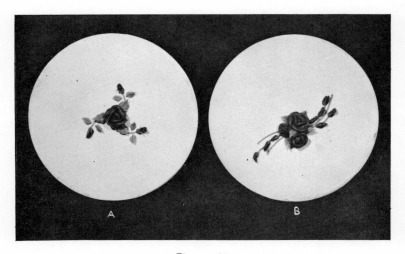

Figure 25

Notes: The difference between formal and informal arrangement should be clear. Notice that the corsage in Figure 25A is made of one large rose in the center and three other elements—stem, leaves and bud—each of which is repeated three times.

On the other hand, the corsage in Figure 25B contains a pleasing variety about a central, unifying formation of three flowers, each of which is different in size.

Duplicate the corsages pictured in Figure 25. Make up variations that are similar.

With pencil and paper sketch some other examples of both styles. When you think you have some good arrangements, try them out with tubes and icing. File good sketches away for future use.

SPRAY ARRANGEMENT

Spray arrangements put more emphasis on stems. Corsage arrangements use stems primarily as a guide for the placing of flowers and leaves. Corsages are sometimes made without using or showing a single stem. (See frontispiece.)

Since the stems are more prominently displayed in spray formations, it is necessary to form them in such a way that they are graceful in themselves.

Tie a string to a toothpick. Press string at center of cake and place point of toothpick one inch from edge of cake.

Mark icing lightly with toothpick as it travels an arc equal to one-third of the cake's circumference. (An inexpensive compass may be purchased at a dime store and used in a similar fashion.)

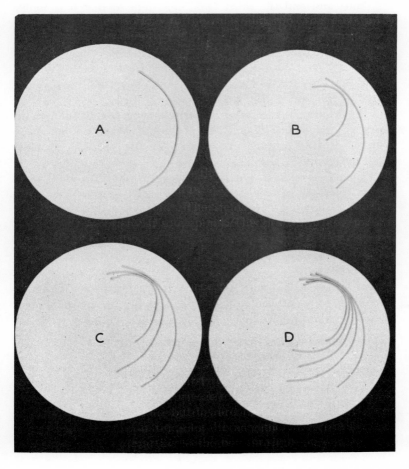

Figure 26

Drop No. 3 stem along curved line that has been etched into icing. This is called the guide or outside stem. (Fig. 26A.)

Starting a short distance below and to the left of the first stem, lead a second (inside) stem toward the first stem, parallel it for half an inch or so, and then curve away from it toward the center of cake top. (Fig. 26B.)

Start and end the third (middle) stem so that it is longer than the other stems. The third stem should be closer to outside or inside stem at both ends of the spray. (Fig. 26C.)

Additional middle stems of any length can be added. (Fig. 26D.)

Working with this basic spray arrangement, add flowers and leaves as follows:

Put a flower at the end of each stem so that it follows the curve of the stem. (Fig. 27A.) Use No. 104 cone and same method as demonstrated in Figure 14 (see p. 40) to make small flowers in Figure 27.

Space flowers on same stem differently and put some flowers to left and right of stems as well as on dead center. Vary shape and size of flowers. (Fig. 27B.)

Put sepals at base of flowers with No. 3 tube. Make narrow leaves with No. 3 cone as demonstrated on p. 29, or make wider-type leaves with small paper V-shaped cone as demonstrated on pp. 41 ff.

Make leaves different in size and shape. Vary their distances from each other on the same stem. Have the leaves come away from the stems at various angles. (Fig. 27C.)

The basic spray arrangement can be changed in numerous ways.

Drop a guide stem as shown in Figure 26A. Drop a short inside stem below guide stem, bringing stems almost together for a short distance toward the center. Drop a long middle stem between the other two, but not down the exact middle. (Fig. 27D.)

Observing same general instructions as outlined above, add flowers and leaves. Each side of spray must be repeated on the opposite side since this is a formal style. (Fig. 27D.)

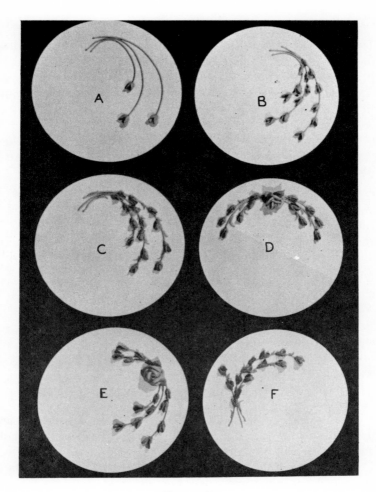

Figure 27

For a different effect, turn cake around. Put writing at top and flowers at bottom.

For an informal effect, cut stems shorter on one side. Use fewer flowers on short side. (Fig. 27E.)

In an upright spray arrangement the guide stem (the one that is equidistant from the nearest edge of a round cake) may become the inside stem (the one nearest the center of the cake).

The other two or more stems vary in length, separation and direction. Observing same general instructions as outlined on p. 60, add flowers and leaves. (Fig. 27F.)

As you can see, there are limitless ways to arrange flowers.

Notes: Certain general rules can be set up as guides at first. As you become more experienced, you will discover many beautiful exceptions to the rules and you will refer to them less and less frequently.

RULE ONE: Have one stem equidistant from nearest edge of round surface. This ties the arrangement smoothly to a round cake.

RULE TWO: The stems at both ends of the spray should be of different length and separation. This avoids an ugly, clawlike formation and achieves a pleasing variety of line.

RULE THREE: One or more middle stems should be longer at both ends than the outside or inside stems. This avoids square, cut-off appearance and adds variety.

RULE FOUR: The stems should parallel each other closely and briefly at some point. This ties the arrangement together; gives it unity.

WREATH ARRANGEMENT

Using a piece of string and a toothpick or a compass, find the center of the round surface and make eight short arcs about one and one-half inches from the edge.

Using the etched lines as guides, press eight small dots of green icing at equal intervals. (Fig. 28A.)

Drop a No. 3 stem so that it curves slightly toward center between the first two dots. (Fig. 28A.)

Then curve it to the same degree between the second and third dots, but toward the edge this time. (Fig. 28B.)

Continue to alternate the curve of the stem.

Starting at the bottom right, make a No. 2 stem come out to the right from one of the main stem points as gradually as a spur

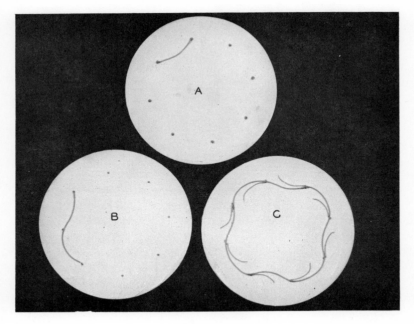

Figure 28

comes off an expressway. Notice that the spurs fill the hollows in the large stem. (Fig. 28C.)

Place largest flowers at eight main points. Place small flowers on small stems. Since this is a formal arrangement, make each section of the wreath like every other section.

Place leaves in a definite pattern which is repeated throughout. Push No. 2 green cone against base of small flower to form sepals. Press No. 3 green cone until bulb is formed at base of each rosebud. Use very small V paper cone to form sepals. (Fig. 29.)

Write an inscription or put a formal corsage in center, if you wish.

Notes: Many other combinations are possible. Additional short stems may be added. Short stems may be used for small buds of large flowers, or they may be used for leaves only.

It is best to visualize the main stem as eight separate stems

Figure 29

(one for each main flower) held together by other twisted stems which are not visible. Always point flowers in the direction the stems are traveling. Notice that the small stems determine the direction of the wreath.

A section of a wreath is often used, especially for a small cake.

The eight-point wreath is ideal for a square cake. A six-point wreath is triangular in appearance and well suited for a small cake. A twelve-point wreath gives a rounder arrangement.

A rectangular cake is decorated easily by using a sixteen-point or twelve-point elliptical formation. The inscription goes in the center. Each corner is decorated with one or more flowers.

BASKET ARRANGEMENT

The basket arrangement is widely used and varies greatly in complexity. Some baskets are simple outlines filled in with stars, latticing, or other designs. These present little difficulty, even for the beginner. The woven variety are more complex and require more study.

Fold a piece of paper or light cardboard. Cut it so that folded edge is two inches long, top edge is two inches wide, and bottom edge is one and one-half inches wide.

Unfold paper or cardboard, dust it with corn starch, and press edges into surface icing. The center of bottom edge of basket should be one and one-half inches from edge of surface nearest you.

Remove paper or cardboard. Trace outline of basket with No. 5 cone of dark icing.

With No. 5 cone of dark icing place marks which divide top and bottom edges of basket into eight equal parts. (Fig. 30A.)

Take a No. 5 cone of dark icing and draw a diagonal line at the left from the first mark of top edge to the first mark of bottom edge. (Fig. 30B.)

Take a No. 27 (star) cone of white icing and draw short

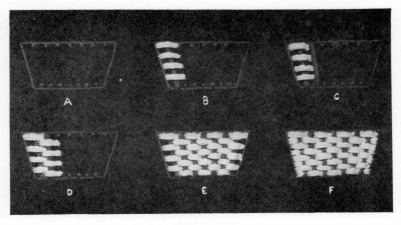

Figure 30

horizontal lines which start at left edge, go over top of dark diagonal line, and stop at edge of imaginary line which joins second mark of top edge and second mark of bottom edge. The horizontal lines must be separated by a space equal to their width. (Fig. 30B.)

With a No. 5 cone of dark icing draw a line from the second mark of the top edge to the second mark of the bottom edge, overlapping the ends of horizontal white lines. (Fig. 30C.)

Insert white No. 27 cone beneath right side of first dark diagonal wherever there is an open space, and bring horizontal lines out and over second dark line to edge of imaginary third diagonal. (Fig. 30D.)

Continue in a similar fashion to complete basket. Notice that the center dark line is the only one that is absolutely vertical. The other dark lines are more or less diagonal, depending upon their nearness to the edge of the basket. (Fig. 30E.)

In order to fill in empty spaces to left of first dark diagonal and to right of last dark diagonal, insert white cone beneath left side of first dark diagonal and bring horizontal line to left edge of basket. Repeat as needed at left and right edges of basket. (Fig. 30F.)

✿   ✿   ✿

Study Figure 31 before proceeding further.

Using a No. 5 cone of dark icing, make a vertical circular motion and "rope" the edges and bottom of basket.

A variation can be made by drawing a base for the basket and filling it in with roping or smooth dark icing. Icing can be smoothed easily with a knife that has been dipped into water.

Cut paper or cardboard the shape of basket handle. Top of handle should be the same distance from farthest edge of cake top as the bottom of basket is from nearest edge.

Etch line into surface icing by pressing edge of paper or cardboard lightly.

Using drop technique, place dark No. 5 handle along etched line.

"Rope" handle with No. 5 dark icing cone.

There are many ways in which basket can be filled with

Figure 31

flowers and greenery. (See pp. 46 ff. for flower nail and apple blossom techniques.)

"Break" straight lines of basket at top and sides by placing flowers and leaves irregularly on both sides of lines.

Have flowers on one side of basket higher than on the other. Avoid pyramid of flowers in center.

If you wish, entwine No. 3 green stems around handle. Place leaves at irregular intervals.

See next Chapter, pp. 72 ff., for instructions for making shell edging.

Notes: If the cake needs an inscription, drop two straight, parallel, diagonal lines of pink icing from one side of the handle to the other. The result will appear to be a white "ribbon" with pink edges. Write message on "ribbon." Or put a "card" made of sugar just back of flowers. See pp. 89 ff. and Figure 45 for sugar technique.

Many combinations of color are used for basket work. Avoid using color of dominant flowers for basket. Colors of basket and flowers should be a pleasant contrast.

A good contrast in basket texture is secured by using a plain tube for vertical lines and star tube for horizontal lines.

Study actual basket arrangements of flowers. Make sketches and put them in your file for future reference. Also file good pictures that you discover in magazines and greeting cards. Keep the paper and cardboard templates that you make. It will save you time later on.

It is time now to explore various types of edgings that will form pleasing frames for our flower arrangements.

V

Star and Shell Work

The variety which can be obtained with a simple star tube is amazing. When the work of this versatile tube is analyzed, however, we find three basic types of stars and two basic types of shells. All the other variations in style and size come from these.

In order to make flat stars, hold a No. 27 or No. 30 cone of white or colored icing vertical to surface. Touch metal tube to surface, exert pressure on paper cone, release pressure and then lift cone away from surface. The result should be an evenly formed star with a depressed center.

If the star is larger on one side than on the other, correct the angle of the cone until it is vertical to surface, before exerting pressure. If the star is not depressed at the center, be careful to touch surface with metal tube before exerting pressure; and be very careful to release pressure before lifting cone away from surface.

If the star lacks one or more points, exert greater pressure If the larger star is unsatisfactory, thin icing and try again. If the star is still unsatisfactory, inspect points of metal tube. Open metal points uniformly and wider with small pen knife, and try again. If the star is still unsatisfactory, check the paper cone inside the metal tube when using the double-cone system. The inner cone of paper must be cut short enough, or it will clog small openings of star tube.

When flat star is being made properly, make rows of different-sized stars, from the smallest to the largest. Make them on the side of a sauce pan or an angel-food cake pan as well as on top. (Fig. 32A.)

If you wish a pin-wheel effect, turn the tube as you press the paper cone. (Fig. 32B.)

With a No. 3 or No. 4 cone of a different color put centers in flat stars. They become attractive, easy-to-make flowers for center, top edge or side of cake. (Fig. 32C.)

The variety of stars, shells, writing, flowers and other work can be increased indefinitely by using two or more different colored icings in the same cone. See pp. 24 f. for suggestions.

THICK STARS

Holding cone in vertical position, place metal star tube one-sixteenth inch or more from surface. Press, release pressure, and then lift cone away from surface. The result should be an evenly formed, thick star with a slightly rounded top.

If one side is too thick, correct angle of cone until it is vertical to surface. If top is rough or pointed, be careful to release pressure before lifting cone.

When thick star is being made properly, try different sizes or other variations as suggested for flat stars. (Figs. 32D,E.)

CONE STARS

Holding cone in vertical position, place metal star tube one-sixteenth inch or more from surface. Press until thick star is formed, and then *lift cone as pressure is gradually being released.* The result should be an evenly formed, cone-shaped star.

If star tilts to one side, correct vertical cone position. If star

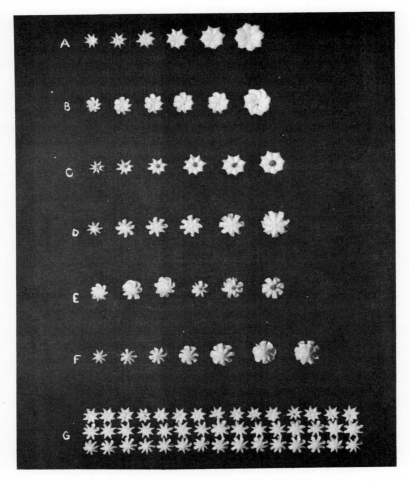

Figure 32

has rounded base, be careful to form thick star before lifting cone. If star does not come to a point, be careful to release pressure gradually as cone is lifted. If it is still difficult to bring cone to point, thin icing so that pressure may be released gradually without having the icing break prematurely.

When cone star is being made properly, make different sizes and elevations. (Fig. 32F.)

The three types of stars can be used to give a picture-frame or beveled effect. Place cone stars at outer edge, then a row of thick stars, and finally a row of flat stars. (Fig. 32G.)

Keep stars uniform and spaced evenly so that they do not overlap or crowd each other. The neatness of this work is what makes it effective. See Figure 49, p. 101, for an example of star work.

NARROW SHELLS

Figures 33A,B,C, represent movement of tube when shell is being formed.

Hold No. 27 or No. 30 cone at a 45-degree angle to the surface. Exert pressure and move cone forward one-half inch at the same time.

Increasing pressure gradually and continuing movement, raise cone three-sixteenths of an inch.

Continuing movement and decreasing pressure gradually, move cone back and down toward starting point.

Stop all pressure when cone reaches starting point. Lift cone toward you.

If shells fall to one side, form loop at lower level.

If shells are wide at the finish and have a rectangular appearance, be careful to decrease pressure gradually to nothing on last third of loop motion. Keep cone at 45-degree angle.

Avoid jamming shells together. They look more graceful when they barely touch each other. Back up one whole-shell space before making the second and each succeeding shell.

Make different sizes at different elevations. (Figs. 33D,E.)

WIDE SHELLS

Holding the No. 27 or No. 30 cone at a 45-degree angle, exert pressure until icing is three-eighths inch ahead of metal tube.

Continuing and gradually increasing the pressure, move cone forward one-eighth inch.

Raise cone one-sixteenth inch and return toward starting

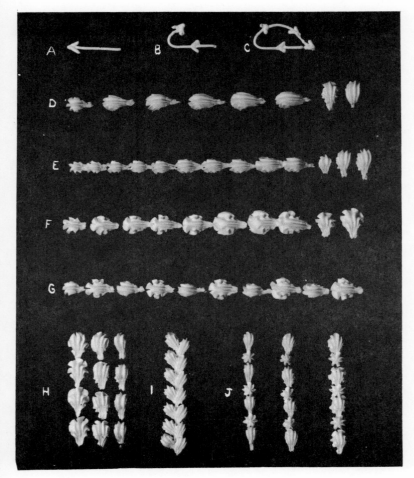

Figure 33

point, gradually reducing pressure. Bring tube to starting point, release pressure and lift cone. (Fig. 33F.)

If shell is not wide enough, press more icing out in front of cone before moving cone forward.

If shells are wide at the finish and have a rectangular appearance, be careful to decrease pressure gradually to nothing on last third of loop motion.

If shells are wide at the base and too narrow at the top, keep loop at a much lower level.

Make a variety of sizes. (Fig. 33F.)

Alternate narrow and wide shells. (Fig. 33G.)

Make an edging of wide, medium, and narrow shells. (Fig. 33H.)

Alternate diagonal direction of small narrow shells made with a No. 27 cone. (Fig. 33I.)

Alternate shells and stars. Make shells first, leaving spaces between them. Then fill in spaces with stars. (Fig. 33J.)

Many other combinations will occur to you as you practice.

Notes: Drill yourself on star and shell work, as well as writing, at each practice session before beginning other work. They are drill subjects. Your style will become smooth, uniform and professional if you drill regularly for ten or fifteen minutes.

Neat edgings enhance the beauty of flowers and other arrangements.

The next chapter will show you many new uses for star and shell work on the edges and sides of cakes.

VI

Side Designs and Edgings

GEOMETRICAL DESIGNS

Geometrical side designs are made up of straight lines and angles. Any inaccuracy in such a design is very apparent to anyone. Consequently, our main concern will be to develop our patterns accurately and evenly.

Place No. 27 stars at eight points equally spaced around the top side of an inverted sauce pan or angel-food cake pan. A Lazy Susan or a turntable is a valuable help. Place one star on side nearest you. Turn pan until star is on opposite side of pan. Place a second star on side nearest you. Turn pan until one star is at your left and the other is at your right. Place a third star in the middle. Turn pan and place fourth star opposite third star. Place stars between the original four. In this way the eight stars are more likely to be evenly spaced. Figure 34 represents the side of a cake or a cake pan.

Place eight stars at base of cake so that they mismatch the stars at the top. (Fig. 34A.)

Put star in middle of imaginary diagonal line between first top star and first bottom star. Repeat. (Fig. 34B.)

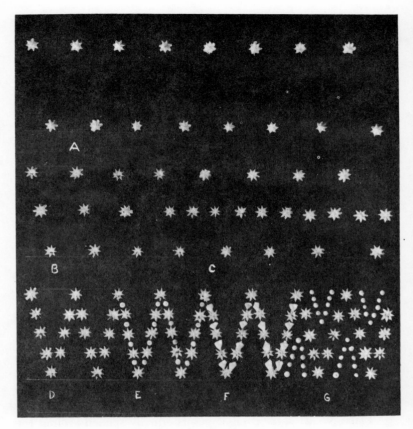

Figure 34

Put star in middle of imaginary diagonal line that runs opposite to the first diagonal line. Alternate direction of diagonals. (Fig. 34C.)

Place stars between middle and ends of each diagonal. (Fig. 34D.)

Put dots of icing between stars. (Fig. 34E.)

Put leaves between stars. (Fig. 34F.)

Make designs within designs. (Fig. 34G.)

See Figures 10 (p. 32) and 12 (p. 36) for latticed design built in a similar fashion.

SCROLL DESIGNS

Scroll designs are composed of curved lines which are made with plain or star tubes.

A *C*-scroll has simple lines and is equally good as side decoration or edging. Reduce pressure gradually toward the end of each *C* and then resume normal pressure at the beginning of the next *C*. Do not stop pressure entirely between *C*'s. (Figs. 35A,B.)

Scroll work may be over-piped with another color from a smaller tube. (Fig. 35C.)

It may be embellished with a variation of "roping" (p. 66) made with a rotary motion, each turn becoming smaller. (Figs. 35D,F.)

The reverse scroll is just what its name implies. (Fig. 35E.) Each part has to be made separately. Both the *C*- and the reverse scroll can be made just the opposite of what you see in Figure 35 by starting at the right and working to the left.

Figure 35

DRAPERY DESIGNS

Drapery designs are especially good side decorations for cakes that are intended for serious and dignified occasions, such as engagements, weddings, anniversaries, birthdays, and the like.

Figures 36A,B,C,D will suggest many designs besides those pictured here. The technique is basically the same. Slant the cone to the right and down as for writing. Fasten the icing, bring the tube straight out from the top edge of the cake and straight back to a point to the right of the original take-off point. Fasten the drapery to the cake before releasing pressure. The weight of the icing forms it into a graceful drapery. (Do not bring the tube down and up. Bring it out from the cake and back to the cake, but always at the same level.)

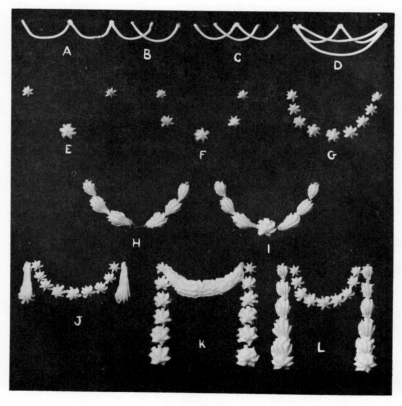

Figure 36

Each section of the design in Figure 36C overlaps the previous section. Make first loop. Start second loop in the middle of the first, and the third loop in the middle of the second.

Figure 36D is self-explanatory.

The draperies in Figures 36E through L are heavier and depend upon techniques you have studied in Chapter V. The cake must be marked in some way so that all the draperies will be the same size when they are completed. The method used for geometric design is suggested. (See p. 75.)

Place two small stars at either end of the space reserved for each drapery. Put a large star between and below the two small stars. (Fig. 36E.)

Place medium stars below imaginary straight lines between large and small stars. (Fig. 36F.)

Fill in rest of drapery with appropriate-sized stars. (Fig. 36G.)

Starting at the top left, curve a line of shells (small, medium, large) down and to the right. Starting at the top right, curve a line of shells down and to the left. Leave a space in the middle where the two lines of shells almost come together. (Fig. 36H.)

Place a large star in the space reserved for it. (Fig. 36I.)

Tassels are elongated shells starting very small at the top, becoming larger toward the bottom and becoming gradually smaller as they return to the top. (Fig. 36J.)

The drapery in Figure 36K is made by constantly moving a star tube back and forth slightly, while gradually increasing and then decreasing the pressure, and moving the cone in an arc at the same time.

The star pillars are made by starting at the top with a small star and then gradually increasing the size of the stars as the tube approaches the base. (Fig. 36K.)

The shell pillars are made by starting at the top with a small flat shell and then gradually increasing the size of the flat shells as the tube approaches the base. A large thick star is substituted for the bottom shell. (Fig. 36L.)

You have studied and used many edgings before you reached this chapter, but here we will review some of the old ones and learn some new ones. You will invent many others as you gain confidence.

Figures 37A through 37D will remind you of the work in Chapter V.

Figure 37H is made the same as Figure 37G, except that a plain tube is used. Try all star and shell work with large and small plain tubes, or with pastry tubes as large as your finger. It is then called bead work, but the techniques are the same.

Figure 37I is alternate star and shell work. Put the shells down first, leaving spaces for stars.

The C-scroll in Figure 37M is made from right to left.

In Figure 37N "roping" is done with a star tube.

Figure 37S is made up of S-shaped links. They must be carefully put together so that they appear to be continuous lines.

Figures 37T and 37U are very simple but very effective.

Notes: Edgings act as frames to pictures. Try to select styles, colors and sizes that will enhance the pictures which you make on the tops or sides of cakes.

Generally speaking, it is a good idea to use large tube work at the base of a cake and small tube work at the top. It is balanced better that way.

Some cakes do not need edgings or side work at all. The sides of cakes can be decorated with cocoanut, sliced Brazil nuts, etc. The icing on the tops and sides of cakes can be rippled with a knife or a clean comb while the freshly iced cake is turned on a Lazy Susan.

Some cakes, particularly those that are covered with a boiled icing, need only a border at the base.

Many people prefer white edgings and side designs. If color is used, it is best to use the dominant color at the base of the cake and less and less color toward the top. An all-white top edging enhances the picture on top of the cake. Small points of color may be added to the white top edging, or white icing may be variegated with a small quantity of colored icing in the same cone. Always turn the tube so that the white icing will be nearest the picture.

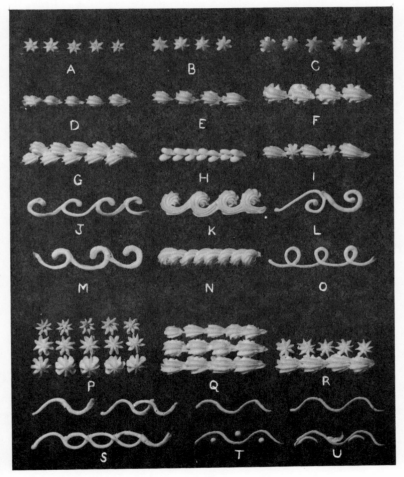

Figure 37

Make the style of side and edge decoration appropriate to the cake. The old rules about unity, coherence and emphasis are still good. If a roping effect is used at the base of a cake, a roping effect or some scroll effect should be used at the top. If a geometric design is used on the side, keep to shells, stars and bead work at top and bottom. Scroll work would not be appropriate in this instance.

It is a good idea to sketch a plan before decorating a cake, especially if it is to be very different from what you have previously done. You will change your plan as you work, but your percentage of successful cakes will probably be higher.

VII

Figure Piping and Sugar Work

HEARTS AND SHAMROCKS

Figure piping and sugar work are valuable additions to a decorator's bag of tricks. Flowers are fine, but for some occasions flowers are not enough.

Most people will be glad to know that they don't have to be artists in order to do good figure piping. Pencil and brush work are two-dimensional art forms. Figure piping is three-dimensional. Therefore, you don't have to learn the difficult art of creating the *illusion* of a third dimension when you are working with icing.

At first our subtitle, Hearts and Shamrocks, will seem a little unrelated. As you study Figure 38, however, you will discover that they are practically the same thing—from a decorator's point of view. They also illustrate the technique that is the basis of all figure piping: Where the work is to be narrow and thin, keep the tube close to the surface; where the work is to be wider and thicker, lift the tube farther from the surface.

Figure 38A is a shell made with a star tube. As the shell becomes thicker and wider, the tube is moved forward and lifted from the surface. As the shell is looped toward you and becomes narrower and thinner, the tube is brought closer to the surface. This technique is accompanied by a gradual increase and decrease of pressure.

In Figure 38B the second shell is started half-way up the right side of the first one.

Most figure piping is done with plain tubes and very soft icing. In Figures 38C,D,E,F, hearts are made in exactly the same manner with No. 5 and No. 3 plain tubes.

The evolution of the shamrock is clear enough except for the last step, which is accomplished by dipping one's finger in water and pressing it against each heart.

Figure 38

CHICKS AND BIRDS

Hold a No. 5 tube in a vertical position and press out a round body for the chick. (Fig. 39A.)

Place the tube half on the body and half to the top left. Press out the head and stop pressure. Dig the right edge of the tube into the head slightly, and then flick the tube to the left to form the beak. (Fig. 39B.)

Place the tube at the center of the body. Make a letter *C* with most of the pressure at the beginning. (Fig. 39C.)

Place a dot of color for the eye. The legs are made in an upside-down *V*-pattern with a No. 2 tube. (Fig. 39D.)

Change the angles of head, wing and legs. The changes that can take place in a chick's personality are amazing. (Fig. 39E.)

✿   ✿   ✿

This type of bird (Fig. 39J) can be used on either the top or the side of a cake. Use a No. 3 tube of very soft icing.

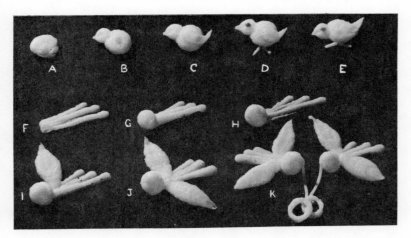

Figure 39

Hold the tube close to the cake and slanted to the right. Run the lines with constant pressure, from left to right to left, three times. Separate lines slightly at the right, but always bring them to the same starting point at the left. Make each line longer than the one above it. (Fig. 39F.)

Tilt cone toward you and gradually lift it as you make a ball of icing at the left. (Fig. 39G.)

Tilt cone toward you and place tube inside upper third of round ball of icing. Start pressure and gradually bring bulb of icing out of round ball of icing. Stop pressure and flick tube to left to form beak. (Fig. 39H.)

Hold tube in vertical position at back of bird's body. Gradually increasing pressure and lifting tube, and gradually decreasing pressure and lowering tube, form right wing at right angles to tail. (Fig. 39I.)

Form left wing at angle parallel to end of tail. (Fig. 39J.)
Birds can be made in pairs. (Fig. 39K.)

PUMPKINS AND WITCH HEADS

Make a letter *C* with a No. 5 tube of very soft icing. (Fig. 40A.)

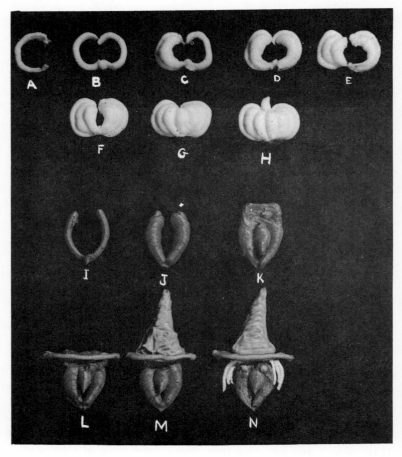

Figure 40

Add a reverse *C* to the original *C*. (Fig. 40B.)

Gradually increase and decrease pressure and gradually lift and lower tube, as another *C* is placed at the left. (Fig. 40C.)

Make each *C* higher than the previous one until the center of the pumpkin is reached. (Figs. 40D,E,F.)

The last section will not be curved, but it will be the highest one. (Fig. 40G.)

Place a stem at the top center. (Fig. 40H.)

*   *   *

Using a No. 5 tube, make an egg-shaped figure with two lines brought to bottom point. (Fig. 40I.)

Put large carrot-shapes at both sides so that they hide the original lines. (Fig. 40J.)

Bring a shorter carrot-shape out from center. Move tube from left to right to left to make forehead. (Fig. 40K.)

Make two or three thicknesses of hat brim across middle of forehead with No. 3 tube. (Fig. 40L.)

Make outline of dunce cap and fill in by moving tube left to right to left, gradually increasing pressure and lifting tube, as it is brought downward to hat brim. (Fig. 40M.)

Add two more layers to hat brim. Add eyes and hair with No. 2 tube. (Fig. 40N.)

STORKS AND BOOTEES

Make an elongated reverse *S* with a No. 5 white cone of very soft icing. (Fig. 41A.)

Place cone at center of *S* and bring curved line to right and down to bottom of *S*. (Fig. 41B.)

Place round ball of icing at top. Fill in body with left-to-right-to-left motion, gradually increasing pressure and lifting tube, and then gradually decreasing pressure and lowering tube. Put tube into center of stork's body. Move tube back and forth three or four times to form wing. Decrease pressure gradually with last stroke to right. (Fig. 41C.)

Overlap two large carrots of white icing to form thighs. (Fig. 41D.)

Figure 41

Form legs with No. 3 cone of yellow icing. Put dots on legs for joints and form three toes at end of each leg. (Fig. 41E.)

Put dot of icing in center of head. Put two long, carrot-shaped lines of yellow icing together to make beak. (Fig. 41F.)

With No. 5 white icing cone suspend a triangle with a rounded base from the beak. (Fig. 41G.)

Fill in triangle with white icing. Start at the top and gradually lift tube and increase pressure toward base. (Fig. 41H.)

Put ball of flesh-colored icing at left end of triangle. Put two small bits of flesh-colored icing at right end of triangle. These will represent baby. (Very small plastic dolls may be purchased in the dime store and substituted.) Put bow of pink or blue ribbon at top of triangle. (Fig. 41I.)

        ❋   ❋   ❋

Bootees can be made with pink or blue No. 5 cone. Make rounded ball of icing for toe by slanting cone toward you. Reduce pressure as you make instep. Hold cone vertically as you make round flat heel. (Fig. 41J.)

Put two circles of icing on top of heel. (Fig. 41K.)

With a very fine No. 1 paper cone of contrasting color make an *e*-scroll (Fig. 37O, p. 81) around top of circle. (Fig. 41L.)

With the same fine cone make a small bow on the toe. (Fig. 41M.)

Make a pair of bootees. (Figs. 41N,O.)

Notes: The icing must be very soft for figure piping. Otherwise, details such as the bird's beak cannot be formed, and items such as pumpkins cannot be formed smoothly.

By using a very small paper cone figures can be piped on sugar cubes and mints. Large items can be piped on cakes and pies by using marshmallow icing, whipped cream or meringue in large pastry bags. Figure-piping technique is the same, regardless of size or material.

SUGAR BELLS

Sugar work requires the use of molds. Once you become interested in this work, you will find yourself collecting gadgets of all kinds. Christmas-bell ornaments, cookie cutters, plastic ornaments and dinner bells will be among them. You may purchase special molds such as the one of George Washington (Fig. 42A) at bakers' wholesale supply houses.

The technique is simple but it requires practice and patience. Put a pound of granulated sugar in a bowl and add a

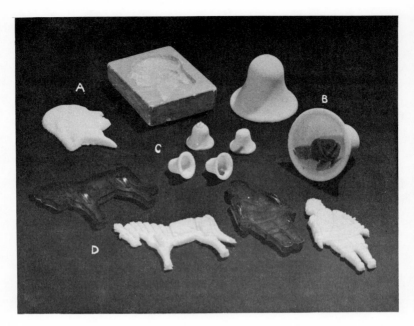

Figure 42

teaspoonful of water. Work the sugar with your hands until it is uniformly moist. Grip some sugar in your hand. If it does not pack enough to keep the imprint of your fingers, add a little more water until it does.

Most beginners get the sugar too wet and then it sticks to the molds. It is better to keep the sugar on the dry side.

Fill a small bell mold with sugar. (Fig. 42C.)

Cut off excess sugar with a knife.

Hold bell with opening one-sixteenth inch above a cardboard or pan. Snap the mold with your finger or tap it sharply with the knife handle. If the sugar falls out easily and keeps the bell shape, the sugar has the right amount of moisture. If it sticks to the mold, it is too wet. If it falls out before it should or does not hold its shape, the sugar is too dry.

When the sugar is right make several bells and allow them to dry for ten to twenty minutes. Then pick up a sugar bell carefully and carve it with a paring knife from the center toward the edges. If it breaks up, let the rest of the bells dry for another five minutes.

At intervals try carving another bell until you learn the proper timing for your batch of sugar under your particular room conditions. If you allow the bells to dry too long, they will become too brittle for carving.

Keep batch of sugar covered with a damp cloth when you are not using it. Now and then it will be necessary to mix a few drops of water through the sugar in order to keep it from becoming too dry.

Take a No. 3 cone of icing and make bell hammer by drawing line from top inside to edge. Finish with ball of icing or silver candy bead.

Large bells (Fig. 42B) are made in much the same way. After the large mold has been filled, packed, and leveled, place a piece of cardboard on top and turn bell mold and cardboard upside down. Lift mold straight up. The weight of the sugar will cause it to leave the mold and remain on the cardboard. It is not necessary to snap or tap a large mold.

The larger the bell, the longer you must wait before carving it. Let the sugar dry for 30 to 50 minutes before making the first test.

OTHER SUGAR WORK

Molds that have more detail should be dusted with bread flour or corn starch. (Figs. 42A,D.) Knock out the excess drying material before packing and leveling the sugar.

If the sugar does not leave the mold readily when the mold is lifted straight up, place a cardboard on the palm of your left hand, and with your right hand slam the mold downward against the cardboard. Place the cardboard and mold on table. Then lift the mold straight up.

Sometimes an individual mold has a particular part that is too narrow. For example, the plastic horse-cookie cutter (Fig. 42D) has narrow legs. Do not pack the leg parts too firmly and the sugar will come out of the mold better. Run the sugar drier when there is a great deal of detail to be worked out.

You can color sugar with vegetable color before adding water. Red and green bells can be used at Christmastime. Pastel-colored bells are appropriate for many occasions.

Sugar place cards or cards for cake tops can be made by rolling out some moist sugar to one-eighth inch thickness, cutting it into desired shapes and letting it dry. Animals and other figures can be made in this way. Use cookie cutters or cut free hand.

More examples of sugar work may be seen in Figures 43, 45, 49 and 51.

VIII

Birthday and Other Special-Occasion Cakes

In this chapter and the next you will see many of the techniques you have been practicing. However, you will see them selected and combined for one specific purpose.

It may be to wish two young men good luck and a safe return as they leave their homes to fight for their country. (Fig. 47, p. 98.) It may be to congratulate a happily married couple on their 25th wedding anniversary. (Fig. 49, p. 101.)

Whatever the occasion, a decorator's main objective is not the perfection and display of skills, important as they are. His primary objective is to select and combine creatively the techniques which will produce a work that will suit the occasion and the recipient.

The examples we have pictured should stimulate you to try out your own ideas. That is when you really enjoy decorating—when you start to create.

CHILD'S BIRTHDAY CAKE

Most children like animals and circuses. (Fig. 43.) This is meant to suggest a ringmaster with a trio of show horses. Some

Figure 43

bright youngster is apt to recognize Santa Claus, who is also a favorite character. The children may be surprised at the incongruity but they will not be overwhelmed. The more "neverlandish" an idea is, the better they like it.

The top of the cake is iced red. In the center is a large sugar bell that has been sawed in half with a sharp knife. A few white stars are piped around the top.

The white and red star ruffles on the legs of the horses keep them from falling over. The ringmaster is braced with two white-iced toothpicks.

The top border is made of large No. 30 white cone stars surmounted by No. 3 red cones. The base is decorated with large No. 30 red cone stars surmounted by No. 3 white cones. (Pp. 70 f.)

Sugar work is described in detail on pp. 89 ff.

OTHER BIRTHDAY CAKES

Figure 44 is intended for a girl who is beginning to feel like a young lady.

The latticed pattern (p. 56) resembles a fan. A folded piece of wax paper is cut, then opened and used as a template against the icing.

The bow is made with a No. 104 flower tube. Notice the wide, frilly shells at the top (pp. 72 ff.) and the variegated shells at the base (pp. 24 f.).

Nail roses are taught on pp. 49 ff.; small flowers along sides of fan, on pp. 40 f., except that a No. 104 tube is used.

The letters are decorated with "roping." (Pp. 66 f.)

Figure 44

Figure 45 is intended for a mature lady who enjoys a well-ordered life. The design is formal and feminine.

The lattice pattern is marked into icing with compass or cookie cutter. A one-half-inch space is left between each section. Each half-moon pattern is iced with light pink icing, and then it is latticed with No. 3 white icing. (P. 56.) Each section is finished with bead work. (P. 80 and Fig. 37H.)

A rose with three leaves is placed in space between lattice work.

Notice the name card made of sugar. (P. 92.) It is braced with a white rose.

The base border is made with three sizes of wide shells (pp. 72 ff.); No. 30 tube is used for bottom row and No. 27 tube is used for others. Leaf cone is used between shells at base.

Figure 45

Figure 46

Figure 46 is for the man of the family. He likes to feel young and usually he likes to go fishing.

The line drawing is easy to do. If the man of the house is not a fisherman, it is not difficult to make a stick drawing of his favorite pastime in place of the scene drawn here.

Bright colors and straight lines are used. An unconventional pattern is best. Dad may appear to be mild-mannered, but he likes to feel a little reckless.

BON-VOYAGE CAKE

Figure 47 is for two young men who are going into military service.

The sketch is simple. The smoke from the stacks forms the message and rolls endlessly around the top of the cake.

Figure 47

The *e*-scroll design at the top is done in white with a No. 27 tube and at the base with a No. 30 tube. The "roping" (p. 66) is made with a No. 27 at the top and with a No. 30 at the base. The whole effect is one of motion.

STORK SHOWER CAKE

The stork cake (Fig. 48) uses the techniques described on pp. 87 f. The bootees are walking around the top of the cake for no apparent reason. However, they do make an interesting pattern.

After the cake has been marked into eight equal sections, the drapery technique described on pp. 77 ff. is used in making the clothesline. The diapers are made with a No. 104 flower tube. They are fastened to the line with No. 2 clothespins.

The rickrack at the top edge is made by moving a No. 104 tube to left and right as it is brought toward the decorator. The bottom edge is made similarly, but the folds of icing are close together.

Notes: You will understand that the photographs make use of dark colors in order to bring out detail for instructional purposes. The "feminine" cakes (Figs. 44, 45 and 48, pp. 95 f., 99) should be done in pastel shades.

The wedding cakes in the next chapter use a great deal of white decoration.

Figure 48

IX

Wedding Cakes

The cake pictured in Figure 49 can be used for a wedding shower, a wedding or a wedding anniversary. Star work (pp. 69 ff.) is used extensively.

The top is covered with stars of all types and sizes in an irregular arrangement. Bows of ribbon are placed at the center. Three large sugar bells (pp. 89 ff.) are edged with No. 27 thick stars and a rose is placed inside of each bell.

Uniform No. 27 thick stars are on top edge. Six roses with silver leaves are spaced at equal intervals. (Silver and gold leaves may be purchased in department stores and supply houses.)

Twelve equal thick star drapes are made as described on p. 79. Tassels are made of stars that become larger and thicker as the cone is brought downward.

The base of the cake is decorated with three rows of mismatched No. 30 cone stars.

Figure 49

TWO-TIER CAKE

If tiered cakes are very tender, large, or high, metal or plastic stands are sometimes used to reduce the danger of breakage while they are being moved. Stands are also used to separate tiers so that cakes can be decorated in a greater variety of styles.

The plastic stand in Figure 50 is made so that each tier can be decorated separately and then assembled later. Metal stands are made on a different principle, but they serve a similar purpose. Various types of stands can be purchased at bakers' supply houses.

However, there are other safe ways of handling tiered cakes if they are not too large or too tender.

Place second tier on a round cardboard that is the size of the cake. Ice cake and cardboard together. Set them on top of first tier after it has been iced.

Still more support is achieved with the following method: Cut sticks of candy as long as the first tier is deep. Push them into top of first tier so that they rest on baseboard or tray that supports first tier. Place second tier with cardboard base on top of first tier and against tops of candy sticks.

Figure 50

Still another way is to substitute sticks of wood for candy. Then you can build the cake higher by repeating the method described in the previous paragraph. As you can see, the object is to have the sticks and the base support most of the weight.

The two-tiered cake shown in frontispiece is wide and low. This is the less formal type. It may be decorated in white, but it is often decorated with delicately tinted roses, leaves, birds, etc.

Four rows of shells are placed on each two-inch ledge, including the baseboard. Four sets of birds are piped at top side of each tier. (Pp. 85 f.) Those on second tier are smaller. The birds are mismatched with roses.

The corsages at base contain a large rose (Fig. 22D, p. 52) with a small rose (Fig. 20I, p. 49) on either side. The corsages between tiers are made with a small rose between two rose buds. (Fig. 22A, p. 52.) The leaf patterns are the same for all corsages.

THREE-TIER CAKE

The three-tiered cake in Figure 51 is high and formal. The hammers in sugar bells (p. 91) are a delicate blue. Roses and leaves between separated second and third tiers are tinted very lightly.

There is a two-inch ledge between the first and second tiers. The top tier is only two inches smaller in diameter than the second tier. The narrow, formal ornament gives the cake more height.

The separation between tiers adds more height and makes possible a different style of decoration. A simple way of separating cakes is to nail two circles of cardboard or plywood to opposite ends of several round sticks. Then cover the stand with icing. Decorate round sticks with stars, shells or beads. Put roses and leaves on base of stand. Place decorated stand on second tier and third tier on top of stand.

A latticed pattern covers top ledge of third tier. The side is decorated with simple No. 3 plain tube drapery (pp. 77 ff.), and small plain beads (p. 80) at the base.

Figure 51

Six buttresses of shell work are spaced at equal intervals around the sides of first and second tiers. In addition to pillar technique described on p. 79, a second column of shells is piped on top of first column. The second layer is started one-third of the way from the top of the first. A third layer of shells is started one half of the way from the top of the first.

Bows at the top of the second tier and ribbons down the

sides of the second and first tiers are made with a No. 104 flower tube. A spot of icing is piped on ribbon wherever a bell is to be placed in order to make the bell secure.

Rows of shells are piped at inner and outer edges of tiers and baseboard to complete the wedding cake.

Notes: The next chapter offers some good recipes for you to try.

After the Recipes are the Calendar of Decorating Ideas and the Index. They will help you find what you need when you need it.

If you have studied and practiced hard since you began Chapter I, you have experienced a great deal of satisfaction by now.

However, you will never be completely satisfied. While your work is winning praise, you will be seeking new methods of doing things better.

You will keep on learning and creating endlessly and happily.

X

Recipes for Cakes and Icings

STANDARD BUTTER CAKE

2 cups pastry flour
3 teaspoons baking powder
½ cup butter or shortening
½ teaspoon salt
1 teaspoon vanilla
1 cup sugar
2 eggs
¾ cup milk

Sift flour, measure and sift with baking powder three times. Cream shortening, salt and vanilla. Gradually add sugar and cream until light and fluffy. Add well-beaten eggs, blend well. Alternately add the flour mixture with the milk, beginning and ending with the flour. Bake in 2 greased 8-inch layer-cake pans at 375 degrees F. about 25 minutes, or in a greased loaf pan at 350 degrees F. about 1 hour.

Note: If desired, 3 egg whites may be used instead of the 2 whole eggs. Double the recipe to make three 9-inch layers.

POUND CAKE

1⅔ cups pastry flour
1 cup butter or shortening
1½ tablespoons grated orange rind
½ teaspoon almond extract
1 cup sugar
5 eggs (1 cup)

Sift flour, measure. Cream shortening with orange rind and extract until very soft and smooth. Gradually add sugar and continue beating. A very thorough blending of the shortening and sugar is essential for a fine texture. Add unbeaten eggs one at a time, beating well after each addition. Add the flour and beat until smooth and well blended. Pour into a greased loaf pan 2¾ x 3¾ x 10½ inches, which has been lined with unglazed paper then greased again. Bake at 325 degrees F. about 1½ hours.

POUND FRUIT CAKE: Add 1 cup chopped citron, ½ cup chopped candied cherries, and ½ cup chopped candied pineapple or 2 cups chopped mixed fruit.

GUMDROP CAKE

2 cups general-purpose flour
1½ teaspoons baking powder
1 teaspoon soda
½ cup shortening
½ teaspoon salt
1 teaspoon cinnamon
½ teaspoon cloves
½ teaspoon nutmeg
1 cup dark corn syrup
1½ cups unsweetened applesauce
1 cup chopped dates
1 cup raisins
1 cup chopped gumdrops
1 cup chopped nuts

Sift flour, measure, add baking powder and soda, sift three times. Cream shortening with salt and spices, gradually add corn syrup and continue creaming until light and fluffy. Alternately add the flour mixture with the applesauce, beginning and ending with the flour. Add fruit, gumdrops and nuts. Pour into a greased loaf pan 2¾ x 3¾ x 10½ inches, which has been lined with unglazed paper then greased again. Bake at 350 degrees F. about 1 hour. Or, bake in a greased pan 2 x 7 x 12 inches at 350 degrees F. about 50 minutes.

MAY BASKETS

    2 cups pastry flour
    3 teaspoons baking powder
    ⅓ cup butter or shortening
    ½ teaspoon salt
    1 teaspoon vanilla
    1 cup sugar
    2 eggs
    ¾ cup milk
      boiled frosting
      small colored candies
   14 pure stick candies 6 to 7 inches long

Sift flour, measure and sift with baking powder 3 times. Cream shortening, salt and vanilla, gradually add sugar and cream until light and fluffy. Add well-beaten eggs, blend well. Alternately add the flour mixture with the milk, beginning and ending with flour. Bake in greased muffin tins at 375 degrees F. about 25 minutes. When cool spread top with boiled frosting and sprinkle with colored candies. Hold stick candy over steam until it becomes soft enough to shape into a basket handle. Insert in cup cakes. Makes 14.

SWISS CHOCOLATE CAKE

    1¾ cups pastry flour
    1½ cups sugar
    3 teaspoons baking powder
    1 teaspoon salt
    ¼ teaspoon soda

½ cup shortening
1¼ cups evaporated milk
1 teaspoon vanilla
2 eggs
2 squares melted unsweetened chocolate

Sift flour, measure and sift with sugar, baking powder, salt and soda. Cream shortening until soft. Add dry ingredients and 1 cup milk. Beat at low speed (200 strokes by hand) for 2 minutes, scraping bowl often. Add remaining milk, vanilla, eggs and melted chocolate. Beat at low speed (100 strokes by hand) for 1 minute. Scrape bowl and beater or spoon. Bake in 2 greased 9-inch layer-cake pans at 350 degrees F. about 30 minutes.

DATE CAKE

2¼ cups pastry flour
1 teaspoon baking powder
1 teaspoon soda
1 cup chopped dates
1 cup boiling water
½ cup shortening
½ teaspoon salt
1 teaspoon cinnamon
½ teaspoon nutmeg
½ teaspoon cloves
¼ teaspoon allspice
1 cup sugar
½ cup chopped nuts

Sift flour, measure and sift with baking powder and soda. Pour boiling water over chopped dates and stir well. Cream shortening, salt and spices. Gradually add sugar and cream until light and fluffy. Alternately add the sifted dry ingredients with date mixture. Add nuts. Bake in a greased cake pan 8 x 8 x 2 inches at 375 degrees F. about 1 hour.

ORANGE KISS-ME CAKE

    1 large orange
    1 cup dates or raisins
    ½ cup nuts
    2 cups pastry flour
    1 cup sugar
    1 teaspoon soda
    1 teaspoon salt
    1 cup milk
    ½ cup shortening
    2 eggs
    ⅓ cup sugar
    1 teaspoon cinnamon
    ¼ cup chopped nuts

Extract ½ cup juice from orange, save for topping. Grind together remainder of orange, dates and nuts. Sift flour, measure and sift into mixing bowl with sugar, soda, salt. Add shortening and ¾ cup milk. Beat at medium speed (300 strokes by hand) for 2 minutes, scraping bowl often. Add eggs, remaining milk and orange-date mixture. Beat at medium speed (300 strokes by hand) for 2 minutes. Scrape bowl and beater or spoon. Bake in a greased pan 2 x 8 x 12 inches at 375 degrees F. about 30 minutes. Pour orange juice over warm cake. Combine sugar, cinnamon and nuts and sprinkle over cake.

PINEAPPLE CAKE

    1¾ cups pastry flour
    1½ teaspoons baking powder
    ¼ teaspoon soda
    ½ cup shortening
    ¼ teaspoon salt
    ¼ teaspoon lemon extract
    ¼ teaspoon vanilla extract
    1 cup sugar
    2 eggs
    ⅔ cup undrained crushed pineapple

Sift flour, measure and sift three times with baking powder and soda. Cream shortening, salt, lemon and vanilla extract, then gradually add sugar and continue creaming. Add eggs, one at a time, and beat until smooth. Alternately add flour mixture with pineapple, beginning and ending with flour. Bake in a pan 8 x 8 x 2 inches at 375 degrees F. about 38 minutes.

APPLESAUCE CAKE

1¾ cups sifted pastry flour
1 cup sugar
1 teaspoon soda
½ teaspoon salt
½ teaspoon cloves
½ teaspoon allspice
1 teaspoon cinnamon
½ cup shortening
1 cup sweetened applesauce
1 egg
½ cup chopped raisins or dates
½ cup chopped nuts

Sift flour, measure and sift into mixing bowl with sugar, soda, salt and spices. Add shortening and applesauce. Beat at medium speed (300 strokes by hand) for 2 minutes, scraping bowl often. Add egg, raisins or dates and nuts. Beat at medium speed (150 strokes by hand) for 1 minute. Scrape bowl and beater or spoon. Bake in a greased 8-inch square pan at 375 degrees F. about 50 minutes.

BANANA CAKE

2¼ cups pastry flour
1¼ cups sugar
2½ teaspoons baking powder
½ teaspoon soda
½ teaspoon salt
½ cup shortening
1½ cups mashed very ripe bananas (4 medium)

2 eggs

1 teaspoon vanilla

Sift flour, measure and sift into mixing bowl with sugar, baking powder, soda and salt. Add shortening, ½ cup mashed bananas and eggs. Beat at low speed (200 strokes by hand) for 2 minutes, scraping bowl often. Add remaining cup of bananas and vanilla. Beat at medium speed (150 strokes by hand) for 1 minute. Scrape bowl and beater or spoon. Bake in 2 greased 8-inch layer-cake pans at 375 degrees F. about 30 minutes.

FRUIT OR JELLY ROLL

1 cup pastry flour

¾ cup sugar

1 teaspoon baking powder

3 eggs

6 tablespoons hot milk

1 teaspoon lemon extract

¼ teaspoon salt

1 pint strawberries, cut fine

4 tablespoons sugar

½ cup whipped cream

Sift flour, measure and sift with ¼ cup sugar and baking powder three times. Beat egg yolks until thick and lemon colored, gradually add ¼ cup sugar and continue beating while slowly adding the hot milk. Add extract. Fold in flour mixture, then the stiffly beaten egg whites to which salt and ¼ cup sugar have been added. Pour in a shallow pan 10 x 16 inches, which has been greased and lined with a greased unglazed paper. Bake at 350 degrees F. about 20 minutes. Sprinkle top of cake with powdered sugar, cover with paper, then turn out on a board. Remove the paper from bottom of cake, cut off edges, roll up and leave until ready to put mixture on it. Cut up berries and add 4 tablespoons sugar. Unroll cake, spread 1½ cups of this mixture on it, then reroll. Garnish top with whipped cream into which the remainder of the berries have been folded.

Note: Jelly may be spread on roll instead of berries.

CHIFFON CAKES

Chiffon cakes have characteristics of both butter and sponge cakes. Melted solid fats may not be substituted for salad oil in these recipes. Egg whites are beaten much stiffer than for angelfood cakes or meringues. Using a long handled wooden spoon for folding prevents overblending. Carefully follow directions for baking and cooling. These cakes remain fresh about a week if stored in cake container.

If using general-purpose flour in these cakes, decrease flour to 2 cups and increase yolks to ⅔ cup.

LEMON OR BASIC CHIFFON CAKE

2¼ cups pastry flour
1½ cups sugar
3 teaspoons baking powder
1 teaspoon salt
½ cup salad oil
½ cup egg yolks (5)
¾ cup cold water
2 teaspoons grated lemon rind
2 teaspoons vanilla
½ teaspoon cream of tartar
1 cup egg whites (8)

Sift flour, measure, and sift three times with sugar, baking powder and salt, sifting into mixing bowl the last time. Make a well in the center of flour mixture; then add salad oil, yolks, water, lemon rind and vanilla. Beat with a spoon until smooth. Add cream of tartar to egg whites and beat *very stiff* or until a knife or scraper drawn through them leaves a clean path that does not go back together. Gradually fold yolk mixture into beaten whites. Fold until just blended. Bake in an ungreased 10-inch tube pan at 325 degrees F. about 1 hour and 5 minutes. Invert pan and cool about 1 hour. To retain maximum crust on cake, remove from pan as soon as cool.

COCOA CHIFFON CAKE

¾ cup boiling water
½ cup cocoa
1¾ cups pastry flour
1¾ cups sugar
3 teaspoons baking powder
1 teaspoon salt
½ cup salad oil
⅔ cup egg yolks (7)
1 teaspoon vanilla
½ teaspoon cream of tartar
1 cup egg whites (8)

Add boiling water to cocoa, blend well. Cool. Sift flour, measure, and sift three times with sugar, baking powder and salt, sifting into mixing bowl the last time. Make a well in the center of flour mixture, then add salad oil, yolks, cooled cocoa mixture and vanilla. Beat with a spoon until smooth. Add cream of tartar to egg whites and beat *very stiff* or until a knife or scraper drawn through them leaves a clean path that does not go back together. Gradually fold yolk mixture into beaten whites. Bake in an ungreased 10-inch tube pan at 325 degrees F. about 1 hour and 5 minutes. Invert pan and cool about 1 hour. To retain maximum crust on cake, remove from oven as soon as cooled.

BASIC CAKE VARIATIONS

Butterscotch: Substitute 3 cups sifted brown sugar for 1½ cups granulated. Omit lemon rind.

Cherry: Substitute ¼ cup maraschino cherry juice and ½ cup water for ¾ cup cold water. Decrease vanilla to 1 teaspoon and omit lemon rind. Before baking, fold ½ cup finely chopped, well drained maraschino cherries and ½ cup fine chopped nuts into cake batter.

Chocolate Chip: Before baking, fold ⅔ cup (2 squares) coarsely grated unsweetened chocolate into cake batter. Omit lemon rind.

Maple Pecan: Use 1½ cups sifted brown sugar and ¾ cup granulated sugar in place of 1½ cups sugar. Omit lemon rind and substitute maple flavoring for vanilla. Before baking, fold in 1 cup finely chopped pecans.

Marble Chiffon Cake: Omit lemon rind. Combine ¼ cup each of cocoa, sugar and boiling water. Stir until smooth. Cool. Pour ⅔ of the basic cake batter into baking pan. To the *remaining* ⅓ gradually add the cooled cocoa mixture. Fold until just blended. Pour this into pan over light mixture. Run a knife back and forth through batter to produce marbling. Or, alternate light and dark batter in baking pan.

Nut: Before baking, fold 1 cup finely chopped nuts into cake batter. If desired, omit lemon rind.

Orange: Use juice of two oranges and add water to make ¾ cup. Substitute for the cold water. Use 2 tablespoons grated orange rind in place of lemon rind and omit vanilla.

Peppermint: Substitute 1½ teaspoons peppermint extract for the lemon rind and vanilla. Just before placing batter into pan, sprinkle top with ⅛ teaspoon (6-7 drops) red food coloring. Fold in with 3 or 4 strokes to streak the batter.

Pineapple: Substitute ¾ cup pineapple juice or syrup for ¾ cup cold water.

Spice: Sift 1 teaspoon cinnamon, ½ teaspoon each of nutmeg, allspice and cloves with dry ingredients. Omit lemon rind and vanilla.

BASIC BUTTER CREAM FROSTING

5 tablespoons butter or shortening
2½ cups sifted powdered sugar
¼ teaspoon vanilla
8 teaspoons hot milk (about)

Cream shortening, gradually add powdered sugar. Add flavoring, then add hot milk until of consistency to spread. Beat until smooth and spread on cold cake.

To improve flavor of chiffon cakes, use a frosting with the same flavor as the cake. Vary butter cream frosting by substituting maple, peppermint or other extracts, or crushed pineapple, orange, and lemon rind, and juice for the milk and vanilla. For chocolate frosting add 2 squares melted unsweetened chocolate.

GENERAL FRUIT CAKE INFORMATION

To cut fruit: Use scissors.

To blanch almonds: Cover almonds with boiling water and allow to stand until skins may be removed easily. Slip off skins. To prevent molding, dry nuts thoroughly before storing in a covered jar.

To line pans: Use unglazed shelf or wrapping paper. Do not use wax paper as it gives an undesirable flavor to the crust of the cake.

For easier slicing of baked cake: Use a wooden spoon to pack unbaked fruit-cake mixture firmly into the lined and prepared pan. Firmly packed cakes are less crumbly when sliced.

Decorating fruit cake: Before baking cake, top may be decorated with citron, blanched almonds, candied colored pineapple or cherries in any desired design.

Storing fruit cake: Remove baked cake from oven immediately, place on rack and cool in pan. Remove from pan, brush with wine or fruit juice. Wrap in wax paper and store in tin container or bread box.

Gift fruit cakes may be baked in covered casseroles or baking dishes. Reduce the baking temperature 25 degrees F. and omit lining of pan with paper. Seal dish with Scotch tape, then wrap in cellophane and tie with ribbon.

OUR FAVORITE FRUIT CAKE
Makes 10 pounds

1 pound currants (3 cups)
2¼ quarts chopped candied mixed fruit, 9 cups (2½ pounds)
3 pounds seeded raisins (8 cups chopped)
1 cup chopped nuts
1½ cups fruit juice or wine
2 cups general-purpose flour

1 teaspoon baking powder
1 cup shortening
1 teaspoon salt
1 teaspoon nutmeg
1 teaspoon cinnamon
½ teaspoon cloves
2 cups sifted brown sugar
6 eggs

Wash currants and dry. Combine fruits and nuts, add 1 cup fruit juice. Sift flour, measure, then sift twice with baking powder. Cream shortening, spices and salt, gradually add sugar. Add well beaten eggs and blend well. Then add the flour mixture alternately with the remaining fruit juice. Add fruit mixture, pack into 3 loaf pans 2¾ x 3¾ x 10½ inches and 1 pound loaf pan 2¼ x 3½ x 6 inches, which have been greased, lined with unglazed paper, then greased again. Decorate tops if desired. Bake at 275 degrees F. about 2½ hours for large pans and 2 hours for the smaller pan. See "General Fruit Cake Information" for cooling and storing.

Note: If using whole candied fruit, chop 1 pound citron, 1½ pounds red cherries and ¼ pound pineapple. Makes 2¼ quarts chopped.

LIGHT FRUIT CAKE
Makes 6 pounds

1 pound white raisins
7 cups chopped candied mixed fruit (2 pounds)
1½ cups short cut coconut (¼ pound)
2½ cups chopped blanched almonds (½ pound)
2½ cups general-purpose flour
1 teaspoon baking powder
1 cup shortening
1 teaspoon salt
1 cup sugar
3 eggs
1 cup fruit juice or white wine

Wash raisins, dry. Combine fruit, coconut and nuts. Sift flour, measure and sift twice with baking powder. Cream shortening and salt, gradually add sugar and continue creaming. Add well beaten eggs. Alternately add the flour mixture with the fruit juice. Add fruit and nuts. Pack into 2 loaf pans 2¾ x 3¾ x 10½ inches, which have been greased, lined with unglazed paper, then greased again. Decorate tops if desired and bake at 275 degrees F. about 2 hours. See "General Fruit Cake Information" for cooling and storing.

Note: If using whole candied fruit, chop ½ pound each pineapple and red cherries, ¼ pound each citron, green cherries, orange peel and lemon peel. Makes 7 cups chopped.

BRIDE'S CAKE
6- and 10-inch pans

6 cups pastry flour
3 tablespoons baking powder
1½ cups butter
3 cups sugar
2¼ cups milk
1 teaspoon vanilla
½ teaspoon lemon flavoring
1⅛ cups egg whites (about 9)

Sift flour, measure and sift with baking powder three times. Cream butter, gradually add sugar and continue creaming until light and fluffy. Alternately add the flour mixture with milk and flavorings, beginning and ending with the flour. Fold in stiffly beaten egg whites. Pour ⅔ of the batter into a buttered pan 10 inches in diameter and 3 inches deep and the remainder in a buttered pan 6 inches in diameter and 2½ inches deep. Bake at 350 degrees F. about 1 hour. Remove smaller cake, then reduce temperature to 325 degrees F. and bake larger cake about 30 to 45 minutes longer.

BRIDE'S CAKE
14-inch pan

12 cups pastry flour
6 tablespoons baking powder
3 cups butter
6 cups sugar
4½ cups milk
2 teaspoons vanilla
1 teaspoon lemon flavoring
2¼ cups egg whites (about 18)

Sift flour, measure and sift with baking powder three times. Cream butter, gradually add sugar and continue creaming until light and fluffy. Alternately add the flour mixture with milk and flavorings, beginning and ending with the flour. Fold in stiffly beaten egg whites. Pour batter into buttered pan 14 inches in diameter and bake at 325 degrees F. for 1 hour, then reduce temperature to 300 degrees F. and bake about 2 hours longer.

WEDDING CAKE
Makes 10 pounds

1 pound citron (4 cups chopped)
1½ pounds candied cherries (4 cups chopped)
¼ pound candied pineapple (1 cup chopped)
3 pounds seeded raisins (8 cups chopped)
1 pound currants (3 cups)
1 cup chopped nutmeats
2 cups sifted general-purpose flour
1 teaspoon baking powder
1 teaspoon salt
1 teaspoon nutmeg
1 teaspoon cinnamon
½ teaspoon cloves
1 cup butter
2 cups sifted brown sugar
6 eggs
1½ cups fruit juice

Slice citron, cherries and pineapple thin. Wash the currants and dry them. Mix all the prepared fruits and nuts together, add 1 cup fruit juice. Sift flour, measure, then sift with baking powder, salt and spices. Cream butter, gradually add the sugar and cream well. Add the beaten egg yolks and blend thoroughly. Then add the flour mixture alternately with the remaining fruit juice. Add fruit mixture and then fold in the stiffly beaten egg whites.

To make a wedding cake with three tiers 14, 10 and 6 inches in diameter respectively, which would weigh over thirty pounds decorated, increase the above recipe three times. Two recipes would make the 14-inch layer and one recipe will make the 10- and 6-inch layers. It seems best to make one recipe at a time and place in pan. Line the pans with unglazed paper and butter well. Bake all layers at 275 degrees F. The 14-inch layer will require about 5 hours; the 10-inch layer about 4 hours and the 6-inch layer about 3 hours. Cool in pans and then remove from pans and take off paper. Frost each layer with a thin coating of butter cream frosting. When assembling layers mark correct position on frosting with empty pans before placing each layer. To transfer cakes slide large knives under each layer and have several persons help lift it to position.

When assembled be sure butter cream frosting is finished as smooth as possible and then allow to dry thoroughly. The butter cream frosting will keep the cake moist and provide a smooth base for the next frosting. Several days before using the cake cover with boiled frosting and when partly dry place bridal decoration on top layer and when nearly dry decorate with ornamental frosting and round and oblong silver beads. Fresh white roses or orange blossoms may be used instead of ornamental frosting.

MARKET LIST FOR 30 POUNDS OF WEDDING CAKE
3 layers—3½ inches deep, 14-inch, 10-inch, 6-inch

3 pounds citron
4½ pounds candied cherries

¾ pound candied pineapple
9 pounds seeded raisins
3 pounds currants
1 pound nutmeats
6 cups general-purpose flour
2 pounds brown sugar
2½ dozen eggs
1 quart grape juice
2 pounds butter
3½ pounds powdered sugar
½ cup milk
1½ pounds granulated sugar

BUTTER CREAM DECORATING ICING
(*Small Batch*)

METHOD	INGREDIENTS	AMOUNT
Note: All ingredients should be at room temperature.		
1. Mix shortening, or shortening and butter, smooth on *slowest* speed or by hand. (At each stage mix batch until it is smooth, but as little as possible.)	Vegetable shortening (Crisco, Spry, etc.), or ¼ butter and ¾ shortening	2 cups
2. Sift powdered sugar and salt (and corn starch if it is used during hot weather).	Powdered sugar	4 cups
Note: Measure powdered sugar before sifting it.		
3. Add *one half* sifted powdered sugar, salt (and starch if used).	Salt	To taste
4. Mix batch smooth on *slowest* speed and as little as possible.	Starch (use during hot weather only)	4 tablespoons (more or less)
5. Add one medium *unbeaten* egg white and flavor.	Medium egg white	1

METHOD	INGREDIENTS	AMOUNT
6. Mix batch smooth on *slowest* speed and as little as possible.	Vanilla or other flavor	To taste
7. Add rest of powdered sugar, etc.		
8. Mix batch smooth on *slowest* speed and as little as possible.		

9. Put icing in tightly-sealed plastic, glass or metal container.
10. Keep icing in cool place.

> *Note:* When stored at a reasonable temperature, 60-70 degrees F., icing will keep for several weeks. Do *not* place icing in refrigerator except under unusual conditions.

11. If icing is too soft because of difference in materials or temperature, add *sifted* powdered sugar.
12. If icing is too stiff, add a little egg white or cold water.
13. Work icing smooth with a table knife or spatula before putting it in decorating cone.
14. Thin icing with a few drops of water when using tubes with very small openings.

BUTTER CREAM DECORATING ICING
(*Large Batch*)

METHOD	INGREDIENTS	LBS.	OZ.
1. Take butter out of refrigerator an hour or two before using it.			
2. Allow butter to come to room temperature.			
Note: If butter is used soon after it is removed from the refrigerator, cut it into small pieces and cream it alone in a small machine bowl until it becomes a soft paste.			
3. Cream butter and shortening together on *slow* speed in small machine bowl.	Butter	1	
	Shortening	2	8
4. Sift dry ingredients together twice.			

METHOD	INGREDIENTS	LBS.	OZ.
5. Stop machine			
6. Scrape mix down with bowl knife.	Powdered sugar	6	
7. Mix smooth on slow speed.	Corn starch		8
8. Stop machine.	Salt		½
9. Add *one-half* sifted dry ingredients to mix.			
10. Mix smooth on *slow* speed.			
11. Weigh egg whites and vanilla together.	Egg whites		5
12. Stop machine.			
13. Add egg whites and vanilla to mix.	Vanilla (variable)		¾

14. Mix smooth on *slow speed.*
15. Stop machine.
16. Scrape mix down with bowl knife.
17. Mix smooth on *slow* speed.
18. Stop machine.
19. Add rest of sifted ingredients (9) to mix.
20. Mix smooth on *slow* speed.
21. Stop machine.
22. Scrape mix down with bowl knife.
23. Mix smooth on *slow* speed.
24. Stop machine.
25. Put unused icing in tightly covered can or jar.
26. Keep icing in a cool place when it is not in use.
27. Let icing come to room temperature before it is to be used.

Note: During very hot weather use 6½ pounds of powdered sugar and 12 ounces of corn starch in step 7 above.

ROYAL ICING
Ornamental icing

2 egg whites
14 oz. powdered sugar (confectioner's sugar)
½ teaspoon cream of tartar
Salt and flavor to taste

Warm all ingredients in mixing bowl by placing bowl in larger container of hot water and stirring constantly until ingredients are lukewarm or about 95 degrees F. All equipment and materials must be completely free of grease.

After warming ingredients beat mixture until it makes a sharp peak when a knife is drawn out of it.

Use less cream of tartar in hot weather. *Keep batch covered with a damp cloth when it is not in use.*

Remix icing from time to time so that it is stiff enough to hold its shape. If icing is too stiff, add a small amount of egg white. If icing is too soft, add a small amount of sifted powdered sugar.

BUTTER CREAM FROSTING

5 tablespoons butter
2½ cups sifted powdered sugar
1 teaspoon vanilla
2½ tablespoons hot milk

Cream butter, gradually add powdered sugar, then add the vanilla and milk until of consistency to spread. Beat until smooth. Frost cold cake.

CHOCOLATE BUTTER CREAM FROSTING: Add two squares melted, unsweetened chocolate.

LEMON OR ORANGE FROSTING: Substitute 1½ tablespoons grated rind and 2 tablespoons juice for milk and extract.

FUDGE FROSTING

2 squares unsweetened chocolate
2 cups sugar

2 tablespoons corn syrup
⅔ cup milk
2 tablespoons butter
1 teaspoon vanilla

Melt chocolate over hot water, add sugar, corn syrup and milk. Heat slowly until sugar is dissolved. Stirring occasionally, boil to 232 degrees F., or until a very soft ball is formed when tested in ice water. Remove from gas flame. Add butter without stirring and cool to 110 degrees F., or until barely warm. Add vanilla and beat until thick enough to spread. Frost cold cake.

BROWN VELVET FROSTING

6-ounce package semisweet chocolate morsels
¾ cup evaporated milk

Combine chocolate morsels and milk. Heat over a low gas flame until blended and smooth. Boil gently about 5 minutes, or until almost of the consistency to spread, stirring constantly. Remove from flame, cool, stirring occasionally, until thick enough to spread on cold cake.

BOILED FROSTING

1½ cups sugar
⅛ teaspoon salt
¼ teaspoon cream of tartar
1 cup boiling water
2 egg whites
1 teaspoon vanilla

Dissolve sugar, salt and cream of tartar in boiling water. Cover and cook slowly until sugar crystals are dissolved from side of pan. Uncover and boil until syrup threads from a fork, or to 238 degrees F. Beat egg whites until stiff, then add syrup slowly, beating constantly, until frosting hangs from rotary beater. Add flavoring and pile lightly on cold cake. If desired, cover with coconut or decorate with melted chocolate.

MARSHMALLOW FROSTING: Add 6 chopped marshmallows just before frosting is thick enough to spread.

LADY BALTIMORE: To ⅓ frosting add ½ cup each of chopped nuts, raisins and maraschino cherries and substitute almond extract for vanilla. Spread between layers only. Frost top and sides of cake with remainder of frosting.

CARAMEL FROSTING

3 cups brown sugar
1 cup boiling water
1 tablespoon butter
1 teaspoon vanilla

Dissolve sugar in water. Cover and cook over a low gas flame 10 minutes. Remove cover, and boil rapidly to 238 degrees F., or until a soft ball forms when tested in ice water. Wrap a damp cloth around the tines of a fork, then remove any crystals that may be on the sides of the pan. Remove from gas flame. Add butter without stirring and cool to 110 degrees F., or until barely warm. Add vanilla and beat until thick enough to spread. Frost cold cake. If frosting becomes too thick, thin with cream.

BROILED FROSTING

9 tablespoons sifted brown sugar
½ cup coconut or chopped nuts
1½ tablespoons top milk

Combine above ingredients and spread on cake while still warm. Brown in broiler under a low flame.

Note: ¼ teaspoon cinnamon may be added if desired.

CREAM CHEESE FROSTING

4-ounce package cream cheese (4 tablespoons)
2¼ cups sifted powdered sugar
5 teaspoons hot milk (about)
1 teaspoon vanilla

Cream the cheese, add powdered sugar, then add hot milk to make desired consistency. Add vanilla. Frost cold cake.

PEANUT BUTTER FROSTING

3 tablespoons peanut butter
1½ cups sifted powdered sugar
4 tablespoons hot milk (about)

Cream peanut butter. Gradually add powdered sugar and then milk. Beat until smooth and spread on cold cupcakes.

PEPPERMINT STICK FROSTING

1 egg white
½ cup crushed peppermint stick candy

Place egg white and ¼ cup crushed peppermint stick candy in a bowl over hot water. Beat with rotary egg beater until candy is dissolved. Remove from hot water and beat until stiff enough to spread. Fold in additional ¼ cup crushed candy. Spread on cold cake.

Note: ½ cup jelly may be used in place of peppermint candy.

"QUICKIE" FROSTINGS

1. Place 3 sweet chocolate bars or a 6-ounce package semi-sweet chocolate morsels on top of hot cake which has been removed from pan as soon as taken out of oven. Spread when melted.

2. Sprinkle grated sweet or unsweetened chocolate and chopped nuts over the cake batter before baking.

3. Beat 2 egg whites until stiff enough to hold their shape, gradually add 1 cup sifted brown sugar while continuing beating. Beat until smooth and thick enough to spread. Fold in ½ cup chopped nuts or grapenuts. Spread over cake batter before baking.

4. Place 16 marshmallows over top of cake batter before baking. Makes enough for one 8-inch square.

Note: Nuts may be added to any frostings.

Appendix

Calendar of Decorating Ideas

New Year's Day

Put a clock face on top of cake. Have both hands point to twelve. Write *Happy New Year* on lower half.

Make drawing of cuckoo clock with cuckoo (similar to chick, pp. 84 ff.) announcing the New Year.

Draw balloons, horns and other noisemakers on top and side of cake. Use bright colors.

Lincoln's Birthday

Shape small cake so that it resembles a log cabin. Make logs with plain tube and chocolate-butter-cream icing.

Decorate a long roll cake with star tube. Make long horizontal lines resemble bark. Put stump in log by inserting piece of cake and then decorating it. Write inscription on log with white or yellow icing.

Valentine's Day

Use heart-shaped pan for cake. Chill cake in refrigerator after it is iced. Fold paper and cut out a heart-shaped template. Press paper against cold icing so that it leaves impression when it is removed. Fill heart with stars or latticing. (P. 56.) Surround heart with roses or other flowers. Make drapery of hearts (pp. 83 f.) similar to star drapery (p. 79) around side of cake. Use lovebirds (pp. 85 f.).

Washington's Birthday

Use mold to make sugar relief head of Washington. (P. 91.) Place it in center of cake. Along top border at intervals place candied or maraschino cherries. Make stems and leaves with icing. Put small flags or shields on top or sides of cake.

Shape cake to resemble a tree stump. Using chocolate icing and a star tube, make vertical grooves on side of cake. Make fine circles of chocolate icing on top of white icing to resemble tree rings. Stick corner of toy, cardboard or cookie hatchet into top of cake. Put candied or maraschino cherries with icing stems and leaves at base of cake.

St. Patrick's Day

Make a border of small shamrocks (pp. 83 f.) or one large shamrock in the center.

Draw a club, tall hat, clay pipe or harp. Entwine harp with small flowers.

Easter Day

Figure pipe a chick or several chicks (pp. 84 ff.) on top or sides of cake. Use a variety of pastel flowers. (Pp. 38 ff.)

Have a chick pull a wagon filled with flowers.

Draw a picture of a cross. Fill it with stars or smooth icing. Use flowers at base of cross.

Bake a cake in egg-shaped pans, or trim cake to egg shape. Ice and decorate it to look like chocolate egg.

Mother's Day

Use mold to make sugar relief head similar to work pictured in Figure 42. Place it in center of cake. Put wreath of flowers around top edge of cake. (Pp. 62 f.)

Make basket of flowers (Pp. 65 ff.) Write suitable inscription on sugar card (p. 92) and insert it among flowers.

Memorial Day

Put crossed flags at center. Place shields or small memorial wreaths around sides.

Father's Day

See p. 97 and Figure 46.

Use easy chair, slippers (same technique as for bootees, p. 89), pipe and smoking stand, newspaper with sports headlines, television set with boxers on screen (stick drawings as in Fig. 46), or anything that depicts his favorite pastimes.

Put the outline of a collar and tie the whole length of a rectangular cake. On the tie write *Father, To Dad, We Love You,* or a similar inscription.

Put a round cake on a round cardboard that is three or four inches greater in diameter than the cake. Frost cake and cardboard with yellow icing. Comb icing (pp. 80 f.) in wavy fashion to give straw texture. Use a flower tube to make a hatband.

Independence Day

Use flags or shields or both.

Place cracked bell at center. Pipe *1776* on it or below it.

Pipe red firecrackers around top or side with No. 5 tube. Pipe skyrocket in center. Write *4th of July* on it.

Columbus Day

Make sketches of his three ships. Use anchor motif around sides.

Make rough sketch of Atlantic Ocean and continents which

border it. Indicate Columbus route to the New World with broken lines and arrows.

Halloween

Make pumpkins (pp. 86 f.) on top of fence. Put witch head (p. 87) between pumpkins.

Put large pumpkin face in center of cake. Make a variety of witch heads around side of cake.

Thanksgiving Day

Pumpkins (pp. 86 f.) can be placed on top or side of cake.

Make rows of corn stubble with corn shocks at intervals. Place large pumpkins in foreground and smaller ones in the distance.

Christmas Day

Place two red sugar bells (pp. 89 ff.) at top center. Arrange holly leaves above them by making rose leaves (pp. 41 ff.) and bringing out points of icing with a damp toothpick. Add red berries.

Draw a candlestick holder. Make flame of candle as though it were a long yellow rose leaf. (Pp. 41 ff.) Put sprig of holly leaves and berries near handle.

Make a spray (pp. 58 ff.) or wreath (pp. 62 ff.) of poinsettia (p. 43) and holly.

Place one or more poinsettias in center. Put pairs of sugar bells with sprigs of holly at intervals around top edge.

Make drawing of fireplace. Hang stockings by using bootee technique (p. 89) and elongating tops against cake.

Make a Christmas tree in the center. Decorate with drapery (pp. 77 ff.), lights, candy canes, etc.

ANY DAY OF THE YEAR

Birthday

See pp. 93 ff. and Figures 43 through 46.

Make lines for staff and proper notes for song. Write *Happy*

Birthday to You under notes. Add name. Put wreath of flowers around top. (Pp. 62 ff.)

If recipient's name is title of a song, use appropriate notes and words.

Make stick drawing of a man's favorite sport or hobby. (Fig. 46.)

Make a merry-go-round cake for a child. Use sugar animals. (P. 92.)

Engagement

Overlap two large hearts on top of cake. Put names in hearts. Repeat design in small hearts around side of cake. Place wreath of roses or apple blossoms, or both, around top. (Pp. 46 ff.)

Use a double-ring motif in a similar fashion.

Use pairs of lovebirds. (Pp. 85 f.)

Wedding Shower

Run short lines across top of cake in a diagonal fashion. Make a garden of flowers at the edge nearest you. Write inscription at top center.

Make outline of umbrella with handle uppermost. Fill umbrella with apple blossoms or other flowers. (Pp. 38 ff.) Have some blossoms falling over edge.

Wedding

See pp. 100 ff. and Figures 49 through 51.

Anniversary

Use appropriate materials (paper, wood, etc.) for decoration if you wish.

See p. 100 and Figure 49 for simply designed cake. Use silver leaves and *dragées* for 25th anniversary. Use gold leaves for 50th anniversary. If you wish, gild various parts of the decoration that are for display only.

Baby Shower

See pp. 98 f. and Figure 48.

Safety pins, teething rings, rattles, bassinet (see basket-weaving, pp. 65 ff.), and nursing bottles can be used as decorating ideas.

Dainty flowers in delicate shades are always appropriate.

Confirmation or Bar Mitzvah

Trim a rectangular cake diagonally at the ends and in a V-shape at the center so that it will resemble an open Bible. Frost entire cake. Using a star tube, make horizontal lines at ends and sides to simulate pages. Use cross or candelabra and other appropriate religious symbols on one side of top. Use flowers and name on opposite page. Decorate top edges of book with small bead work. (P. 80.) Using flower tube, make flat ribbon of icing around base to resemble edges of book covers.

Graduation

Roll up a piece of paper so that it looks like a diploma. Tie ribbons (school colors) at center.

Make a simple drawing of an owl with a graduation hat on his head, glasses on his nose and a book under his wing.

Sketch a graduation hat with tassel of school colors. Or make one, using a gumdrop and piece of cardboard.

Congratulations

Imitate the lettering and style of a telegram on a rectangular cake. Use flowers around base of cake. This idea can be used for birthdays, anniversaries, retirement, and other appropriate occasions.

Bon Voyage

See pp. 97 f. and Figure 47.

A design of anchors and lifesavers can be used.

If the recipient is making a train trip, sketch an old-fashioned locomotive. Use plane or automobile sketch if either one happens to be appropriate.

Use horseshoe design. Write inscription on design or in the middle of the cake. Weave a garland of small flowers about the horseshoe.

Meet the Author

Richard V. Snyder, A.B., A.M., owner and instructor of the Snyder School of Cake Decoration of Detroit, not only teaches hobby and professional classes in the art of cake decoration in his private school, but he is also currently an instructor of commercial baking at the Chadsey High School. He has appeared on local television programs, and his work has been given considerable publicity in Detroit newspapers.

Earlier, he taught high school English for four years, was pastry chef and food steward on Great Lakes cruisers for three summers; from 1944 to 1946 he was a naval officer on active duty, serving on the aircraft carrier *Shangri-La* off Okinawa and Japan. He holds both a Michigan Teachers' Life Certificate and a Permanent Smith-Hughes Trade Certificate.

Index

35; recipes, *see* Recipes for cakes and icings; writing with, *see* Writing with icing
Imaginative flowers, 39–41
Independence Day cake, 131
Informal corsage, 57–58

J

Jelly roll RECIPE, 112

K

Kiss-Me Cake, Orange, RECIPE, 110

L

Latticing, 56
Lazy Susan, 34
Leaves, 29, 41–43; narrow, 29; wide, 41; ridged, 42
Lemon or basic chiffon cake RECIPE, 113
Lemon (or orange) buttercream frosting RECIPE, 124
Lettering, *see* Writing
Light fruit cake RECIPE, 117–18
Lilies of the valley, 43–46
Lincoln's Birthday cake, 129
Lining pans, 116
Lovebirds, 85–86

M

Man's cake, 97
Maple-pecan chiffon cake RECIPE, 115
Marble chiffon cake REC., 115
Market list for 30 pounds of wedding cake, 120–21

Materials and tools, 13
May baskets (cake) RECIPE, 108
Memorial Day cake, 131
Metal tubes, how to use, 18–20; where to buy, 19
Molds for sugar, how to use, 89–92
Mother's Day cake, 131

N

Nail roses, 49–53
Nails for flower-making, 46, 49
Narrow shells, 72
New Year's Day cake, 129
Nut chiffon cake RECIPE, 115

O

One-tier (wedding) cake, 100–101
Orange (or lemon) buttercream frosting RECIPE, 124
Orange chiffon cake RECIPE, 115
Orange Kiss-Me Cake RECIPE, 110
Ornamental icing (Royal Icing), 124
Overpiped scroll, 77

P

Pans, lining, 116
Pansies, 48
Paper cones, how to make, 15–18